Kathy LeSage

ONE WOMAN'S MONTANA

PHOTOGRAPHS

RIVERBEND PUBLISHING
P.O. Box 5833
Helena, MT 59604
Toll-free 1-866-787-2363
www.riverbendpublishing.com

Published by Riverbend Publishing, Helena, Montana

Printed in South Korea

1 2 3 4 5 6 7 8 9 SI 15 14 13 12 11 10 09 08 07

Cover and text design by DD Dowden

ISBN 10: 1-931832-88-9
ISBN 13: 978-1-931832-88-5

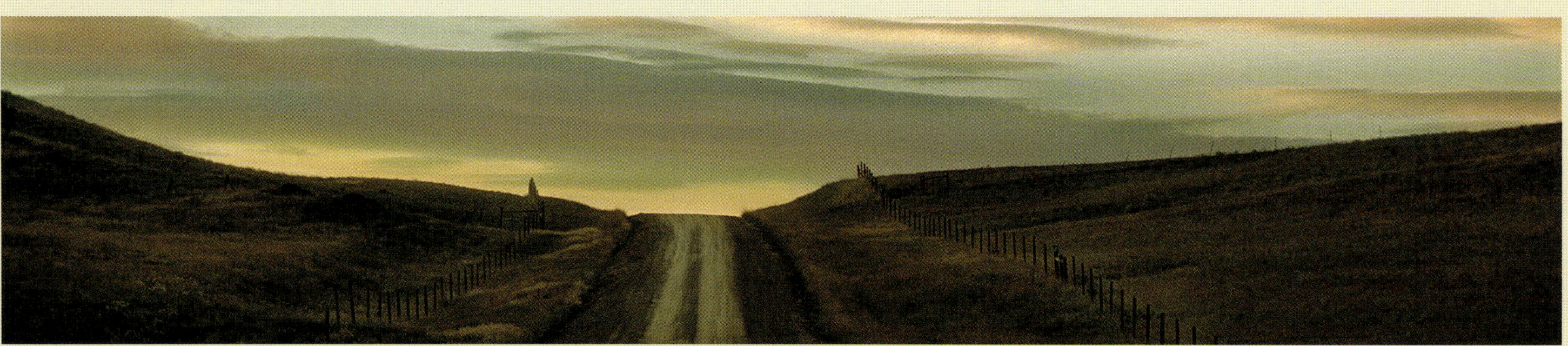

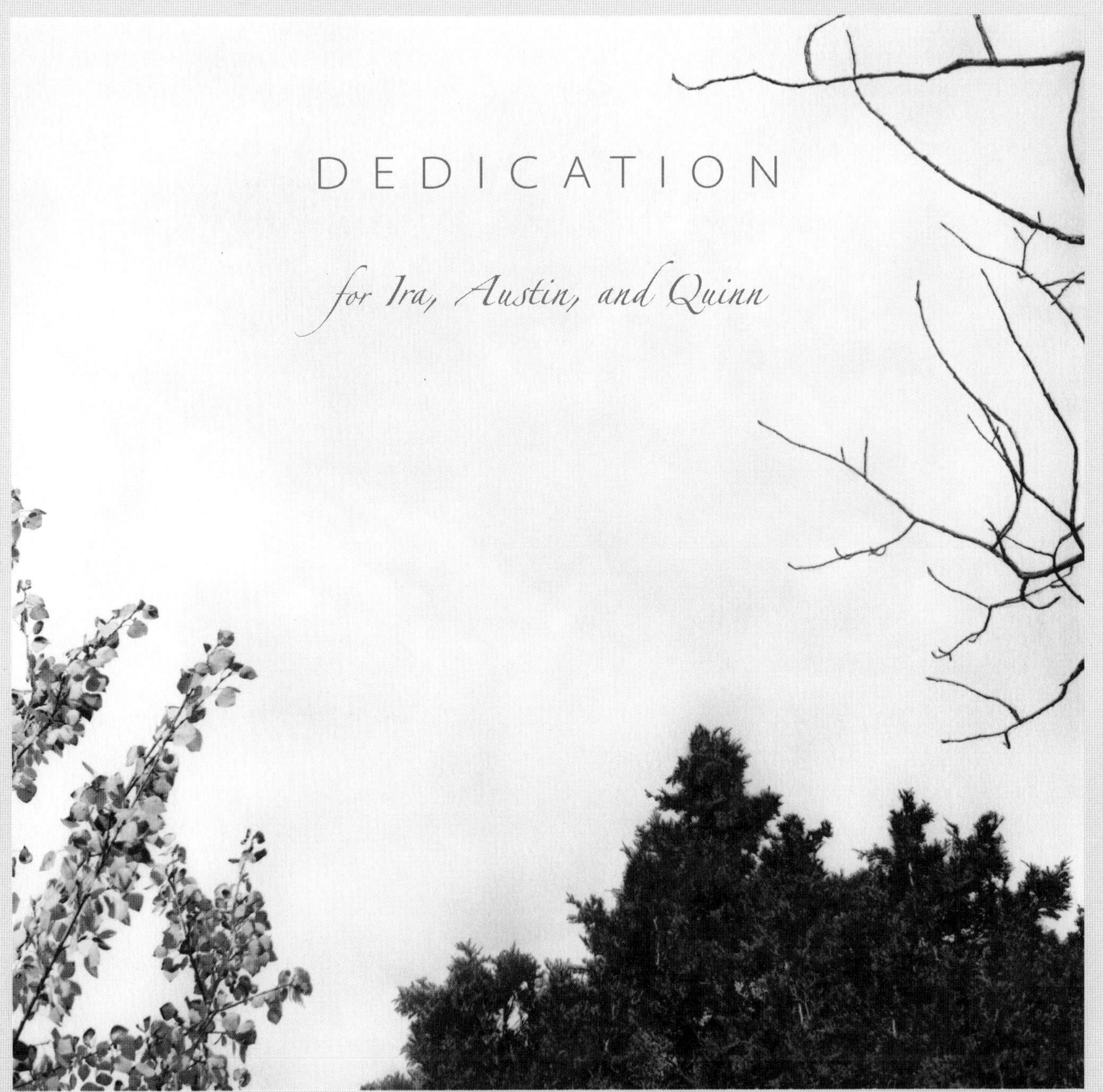

DEDICATION

for Ira, Austin, and Quinn

PREFACE

Lazy, thick, pink light slides down the ridge at the same pace the clouds are dancing east. It will touch and alter the grass near my feet very soon. My toes feel the color through my shoes. This light reaches for the old deer bones in the leaves. Their beauty becomes amplified, illuminated—the greens and pinks of weather and age, the porous textures, the sculptural curves and grooves cradled and framed by fallen chokecherry leaves. How many shades of pink, orange, red, green, and yellow are there, all given new life in this light? The imperfect becomes perfect in the balance of form, proximity, and touch. This unified offering is a gift born of the alchemy of seasons, time, light, life, discovery, death, and the receipt of attention. I watch, and I photograph.

I was born in Great Falls, Montana, from somewhere that had shaped me already. At age seven, my family moved to the mountains near Bozeman, a perfect playground with all the elements that a natural environment provides. Early on there was a thought, a hint, a sensing that there is more at play than meets the eye. I'd felt this certainty very early and mainly when outside, usually alone in the woods or by the creek. Over time this knowing was joined by the understanding that where attention is placed, creation occurs. Then came a sense of responsibility and some questions. What do I want to create? What do I want to add? Where shall my attention be placed? On beauty, harmony, joy, balance—love.

My early certainty and later understanding meld together and serve as rebar through my life, photography in particular. For me, photography is magical—a perfect pairing that allows exploration and communion. Photography records the vibrations of the visible spectrum. By its very nature, a photograph is more believable than other art forms. This fact underscores my interest: the visible with the unseen. I feel inspired to conduct my own relations with the unseen energy behind creation, so for me, photography becomes conversational: visual listening and discussion—working my will but being willing to collaborate and co-create—a receipt and a taking. A precise pattern in life occurs only once and may be interpretively captured in a still photograph. I'm at my photographic happiest when this event feels self-choreographed, when I am a participant and a witness. Collecting and reflecting these moments of interconnectedness, the lowest common denominator of creation, the energy of creation—this is the subject of my attention. The beauty, the harmony, the joy, the balance—the love.

It is more than fascinating when all comes together: the seeing—visual listening—collaborative choreography—discovery—the sciences—technical choices with fidelity to the original while allowing the freedom of intuitive interpretation. As a visual artist, I wonder at the created world and the creative world—being part of these—choosing work to do—loving that work. Isn't that enough to fill anyone with wonder?

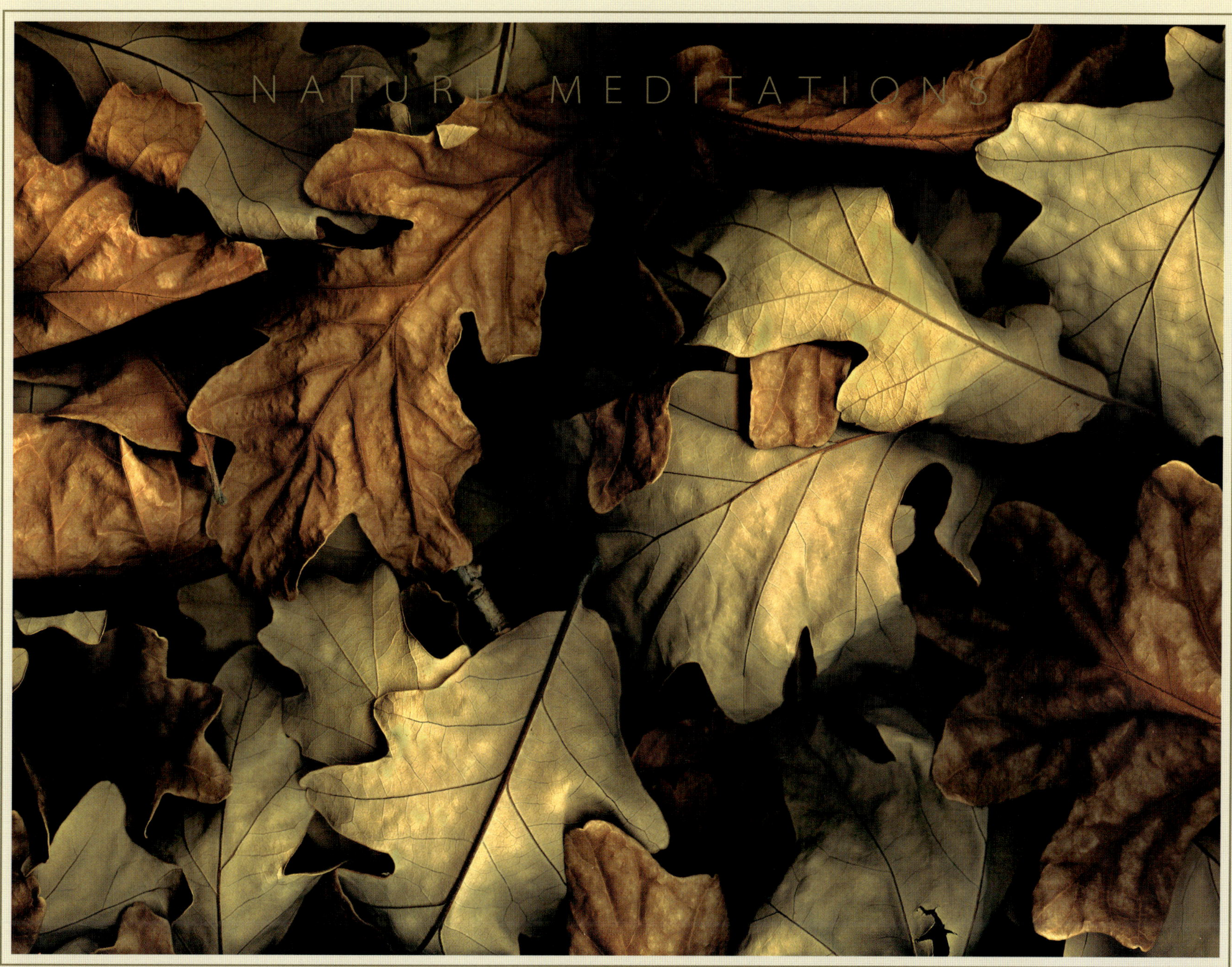
NATURE MEDITATIONS

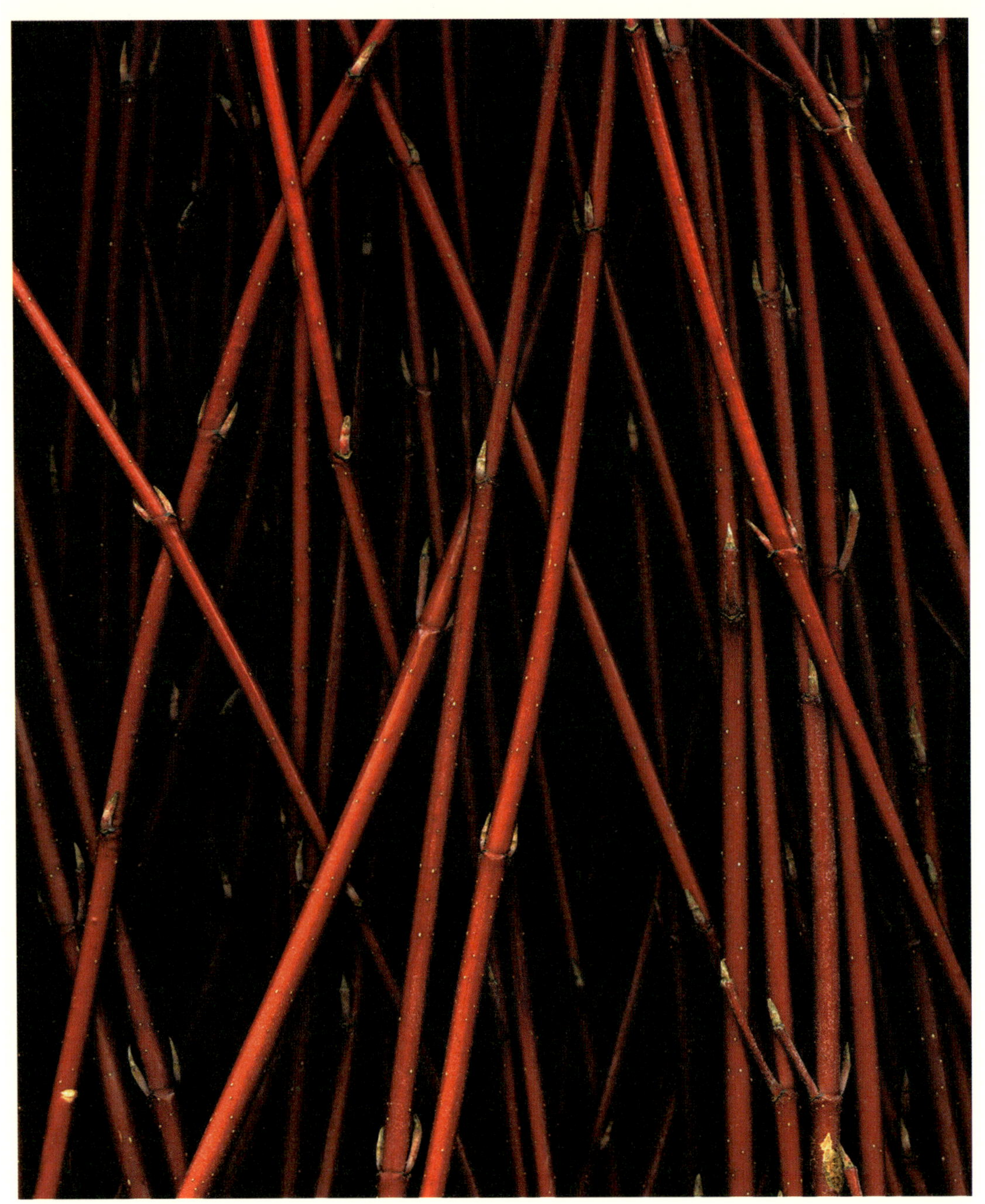

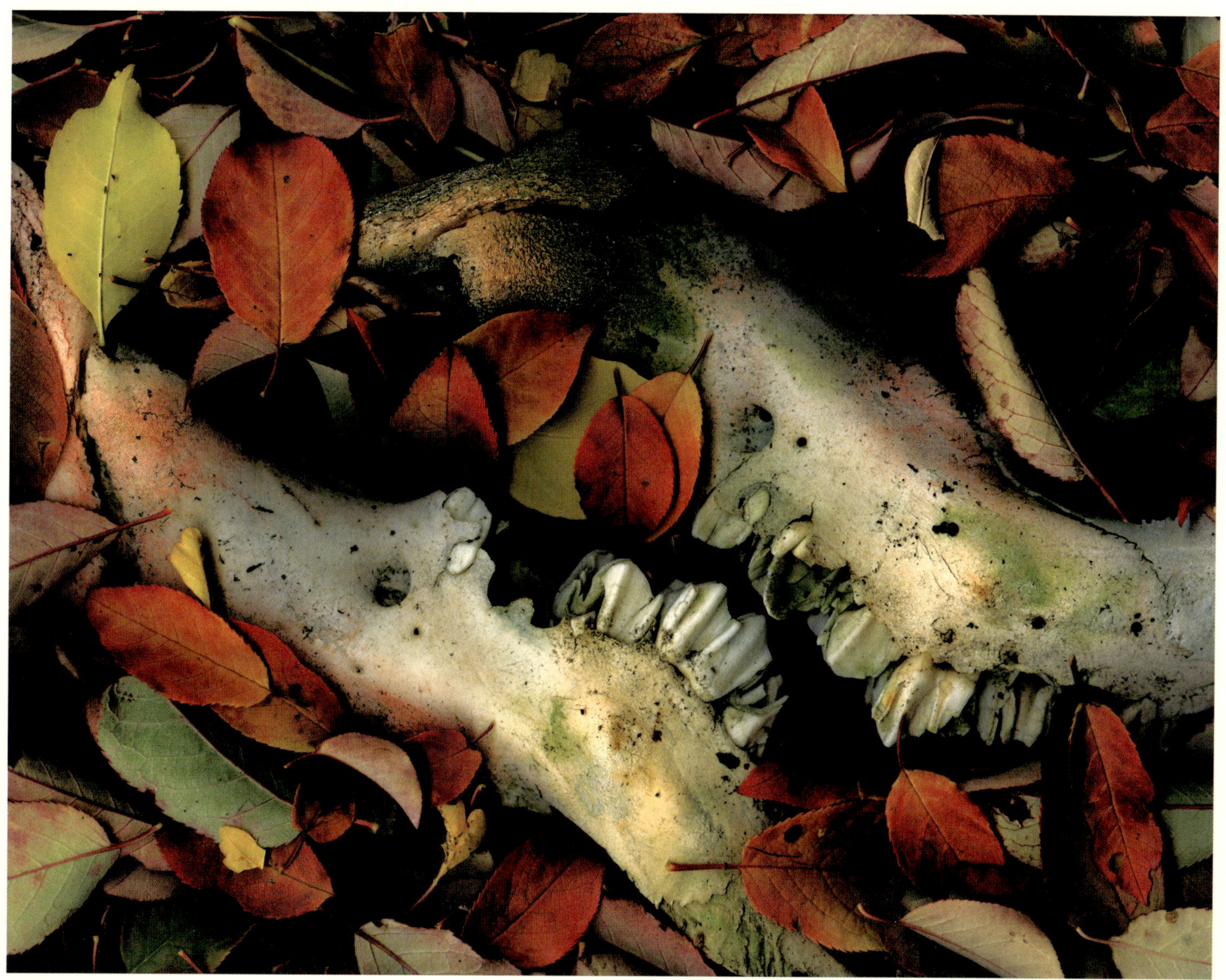

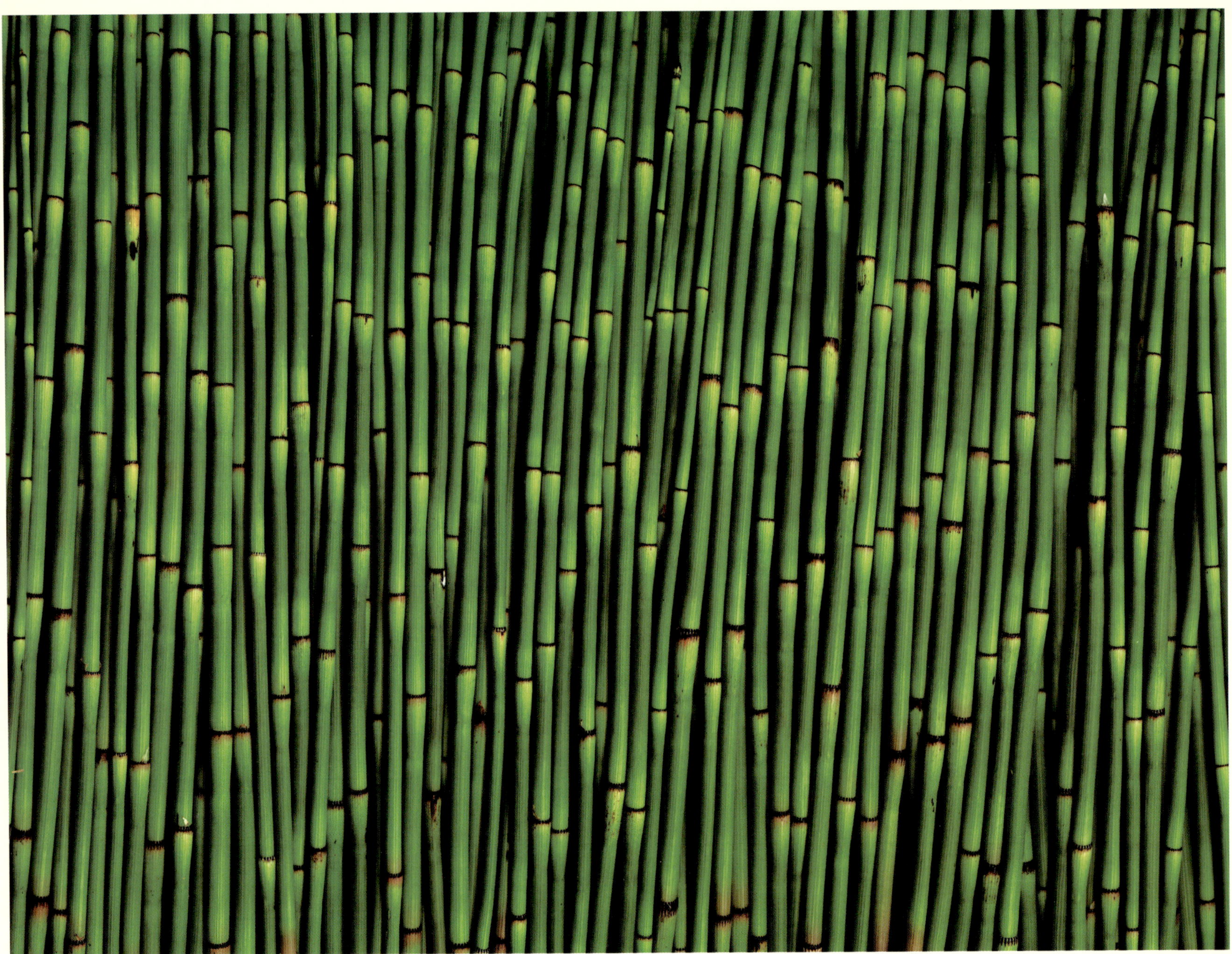

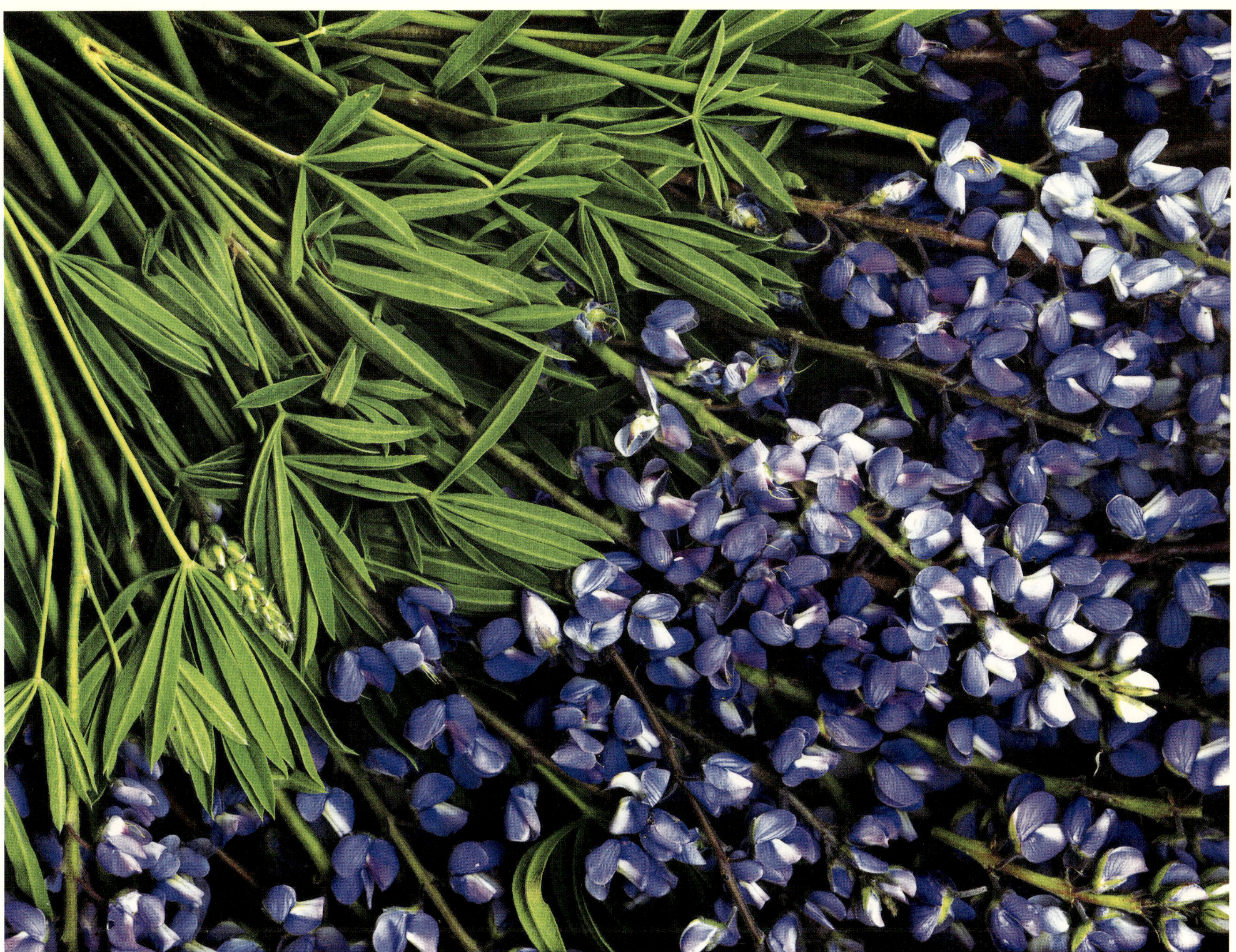

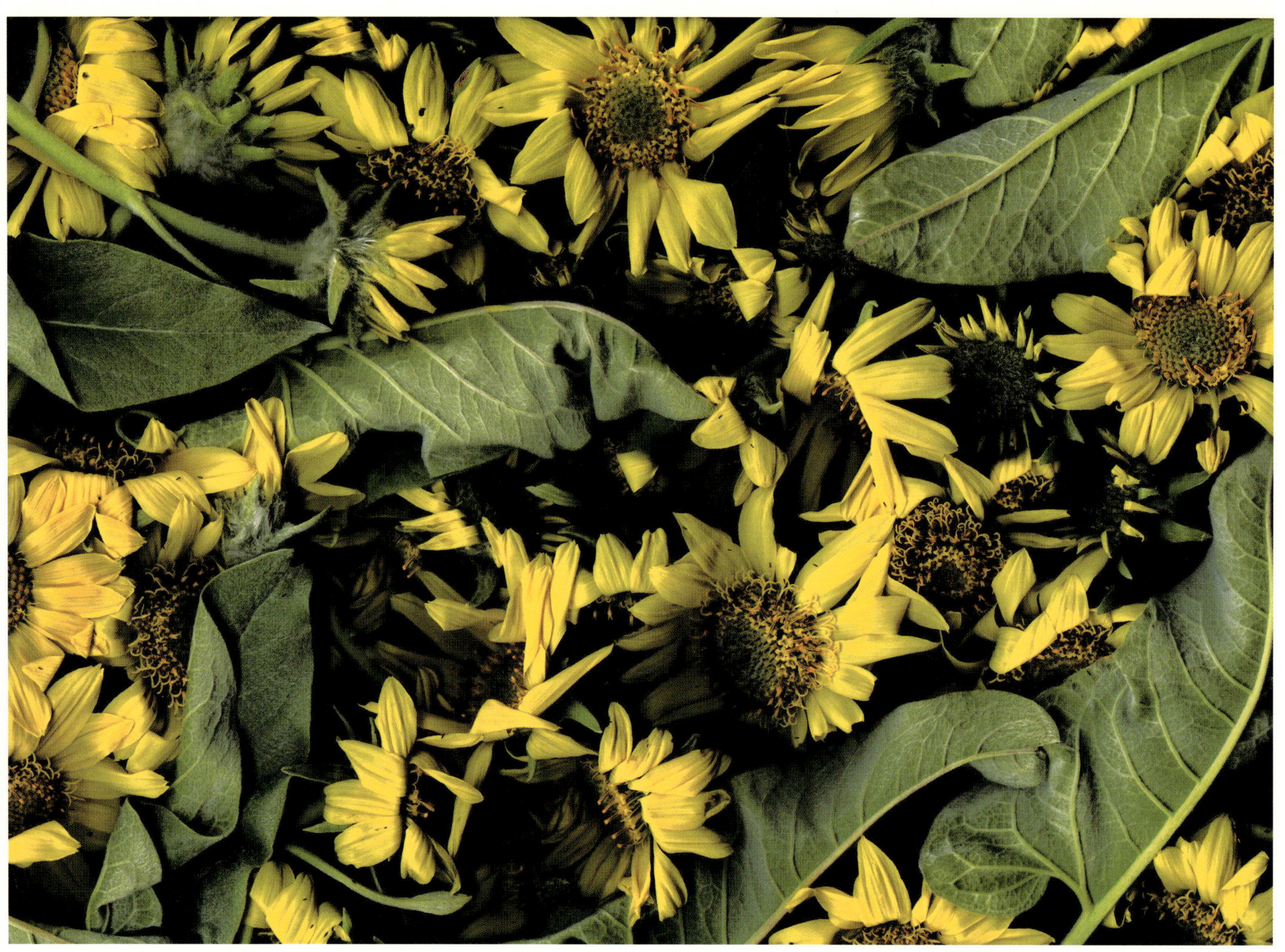

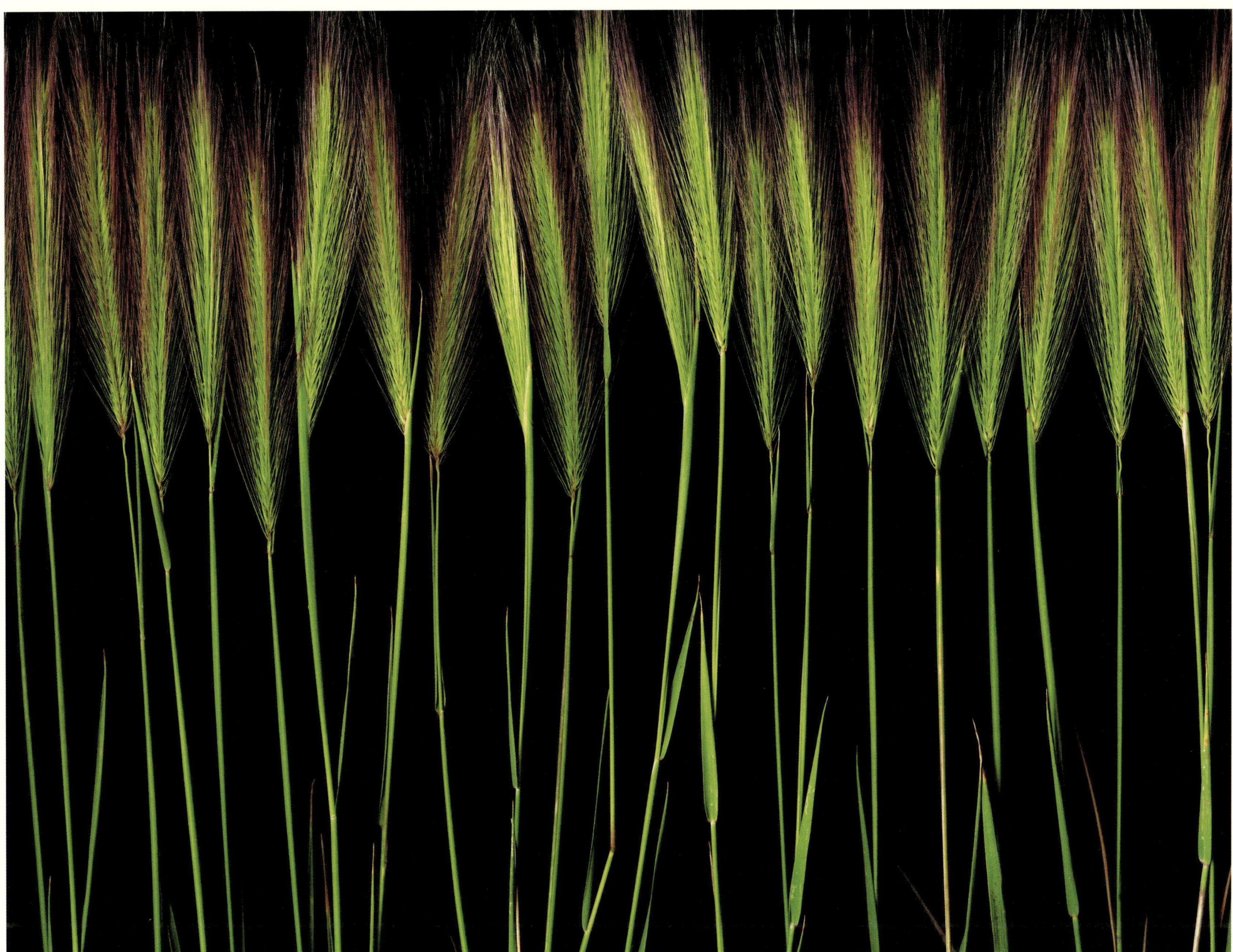

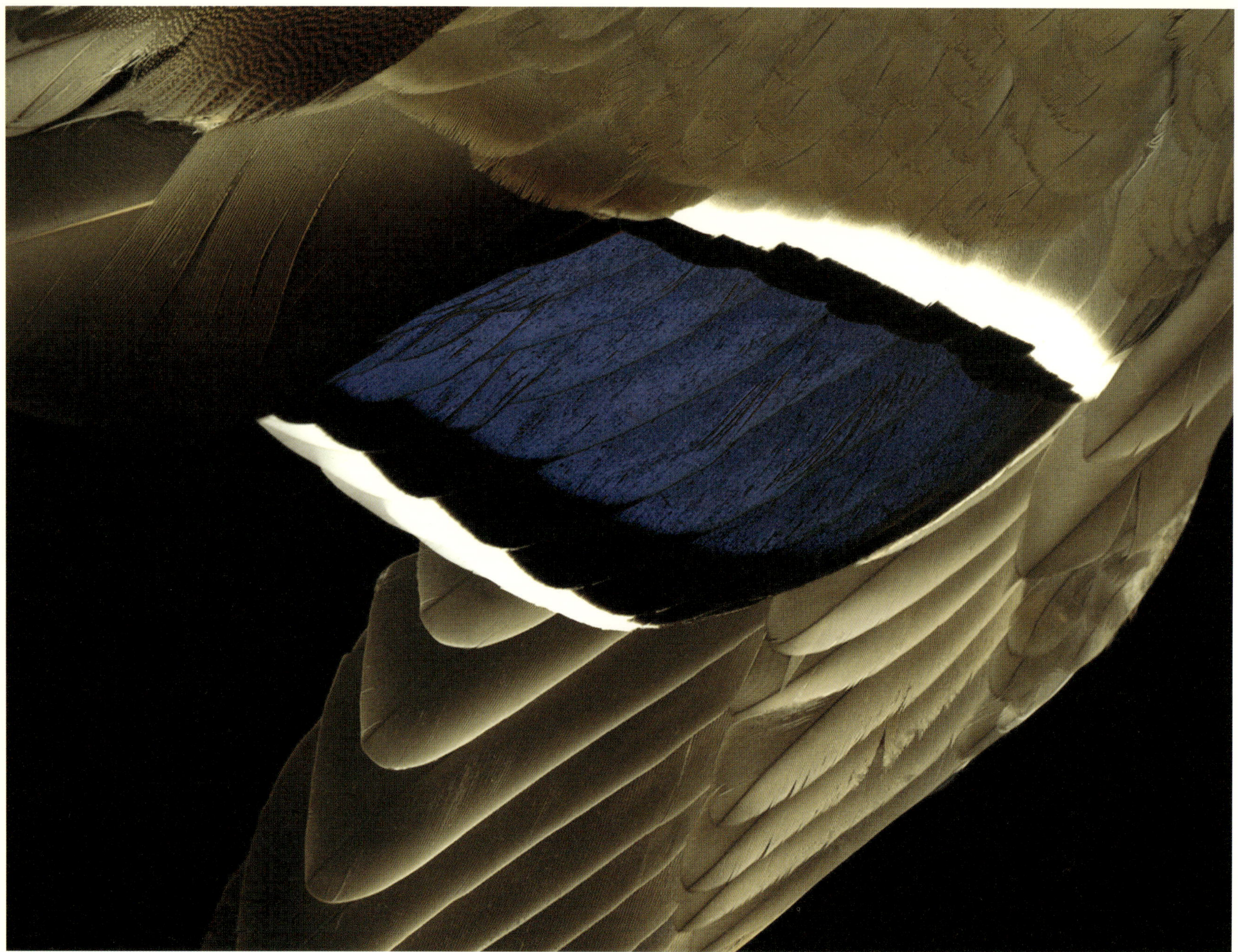

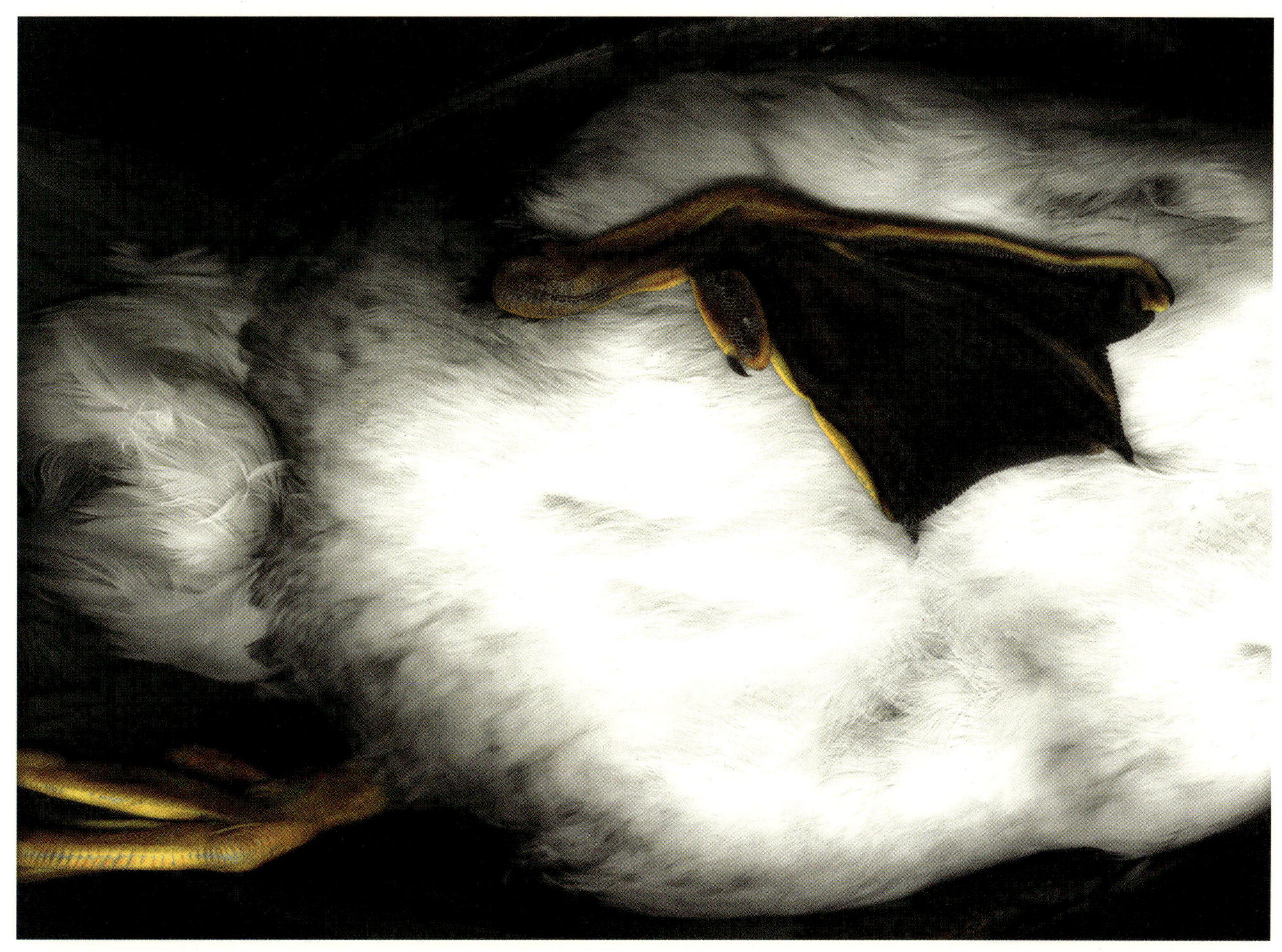

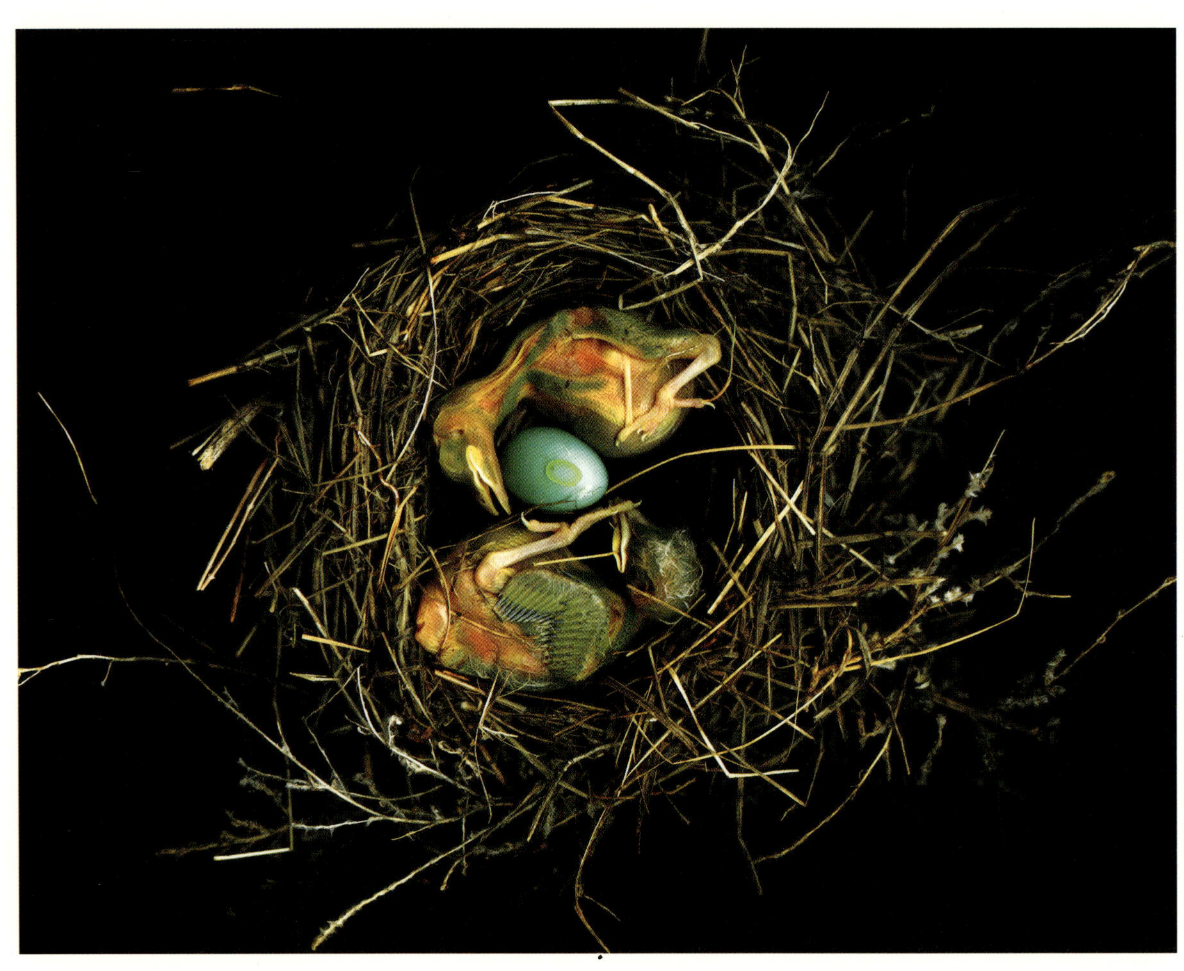

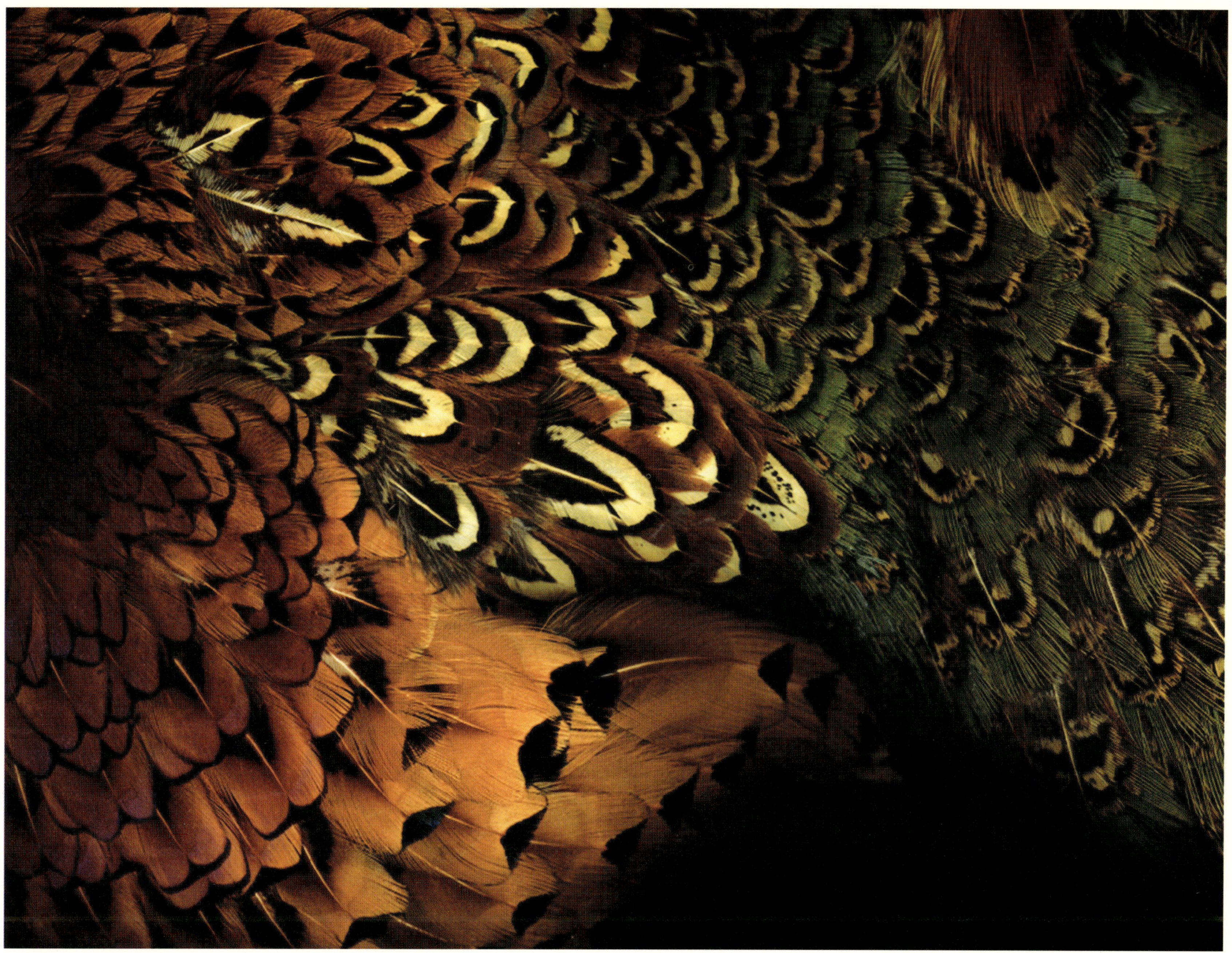

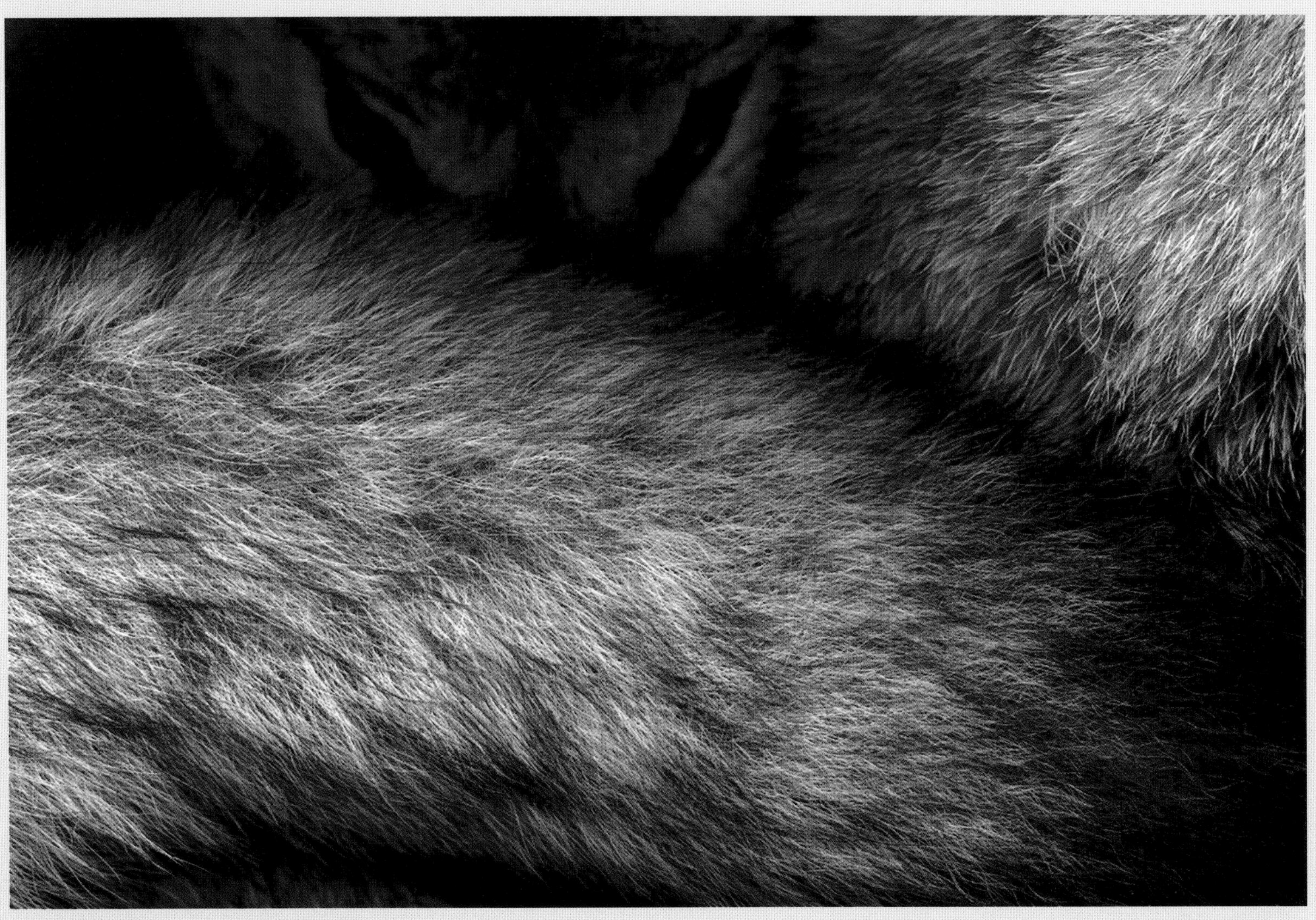

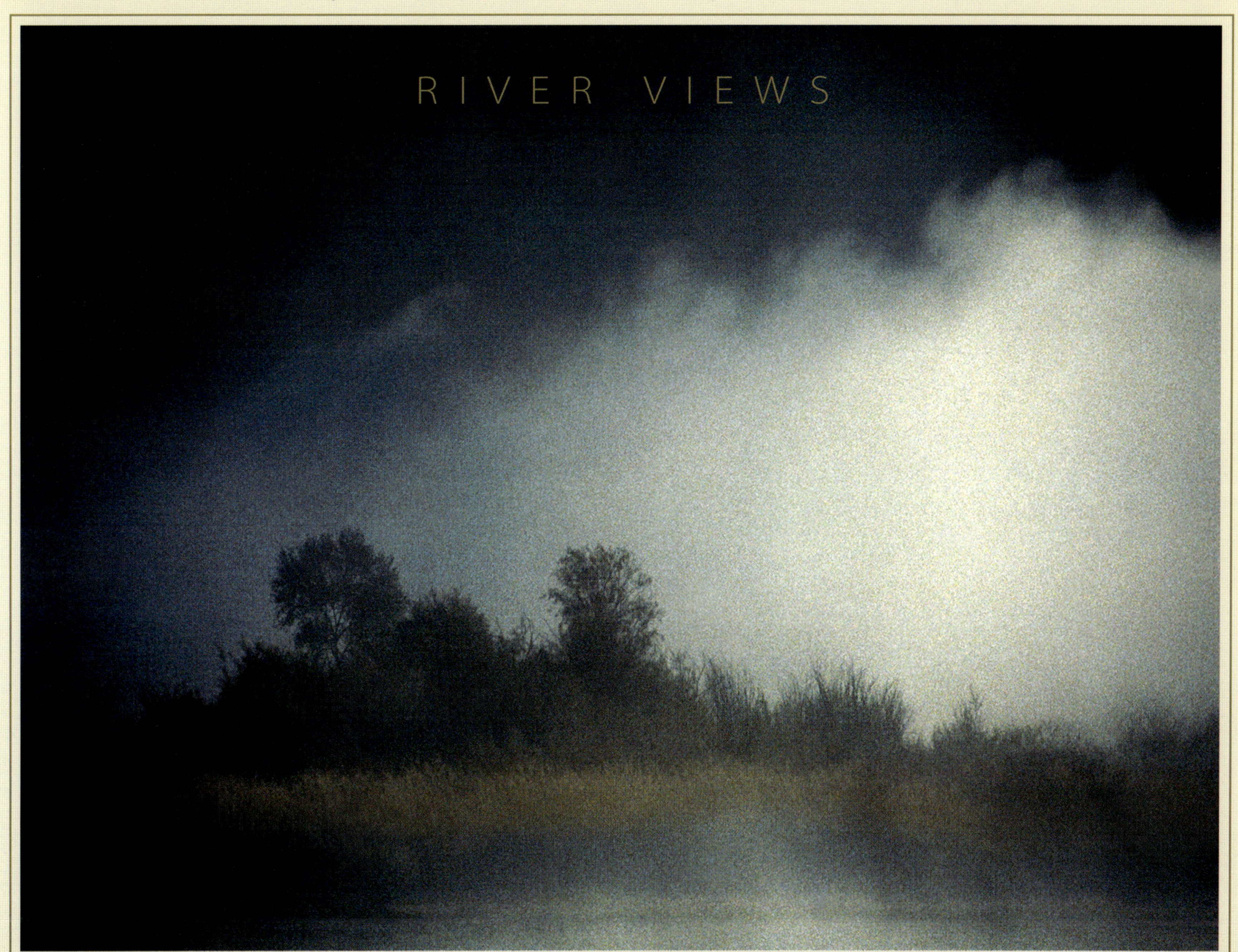
RIVER VIEWS

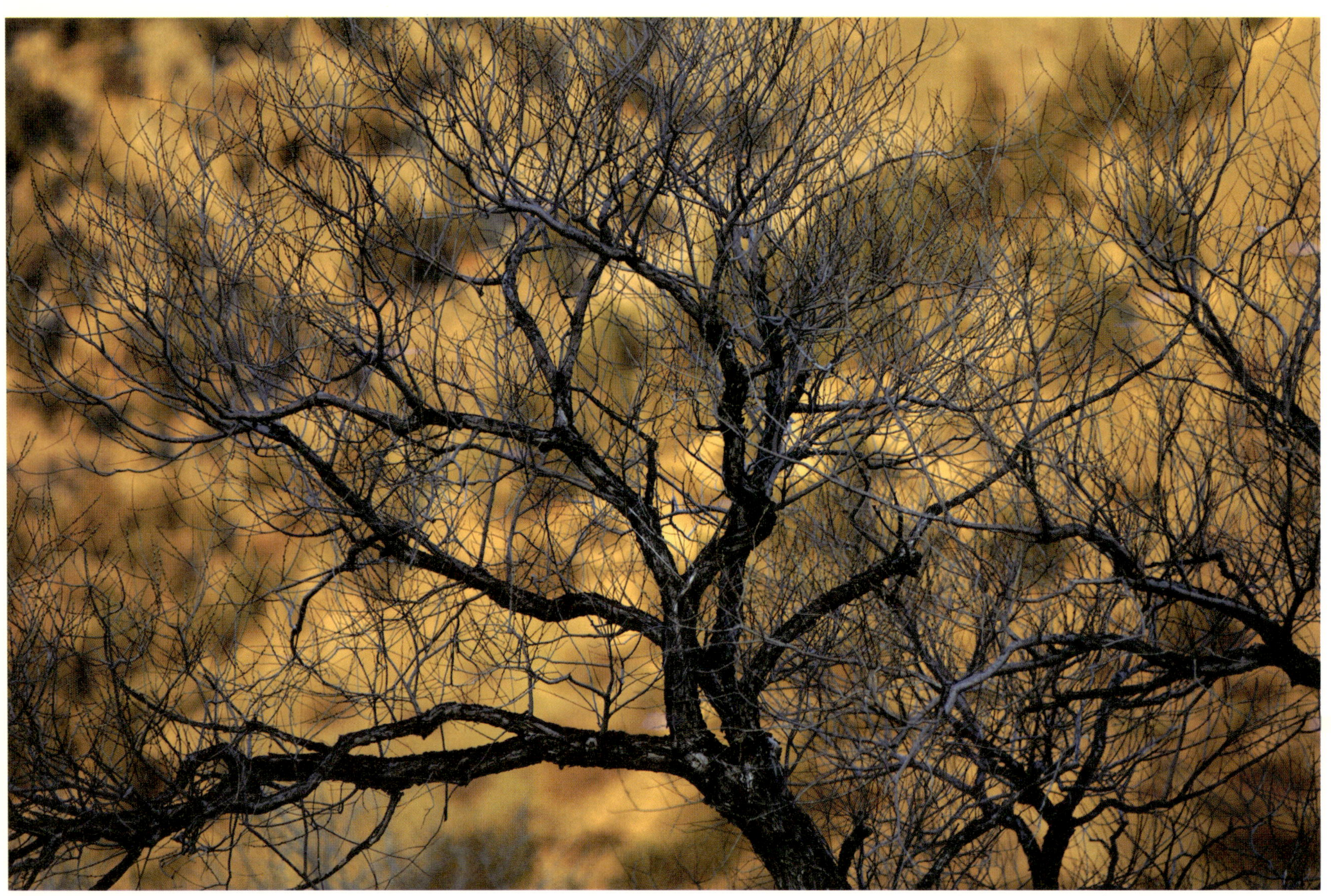

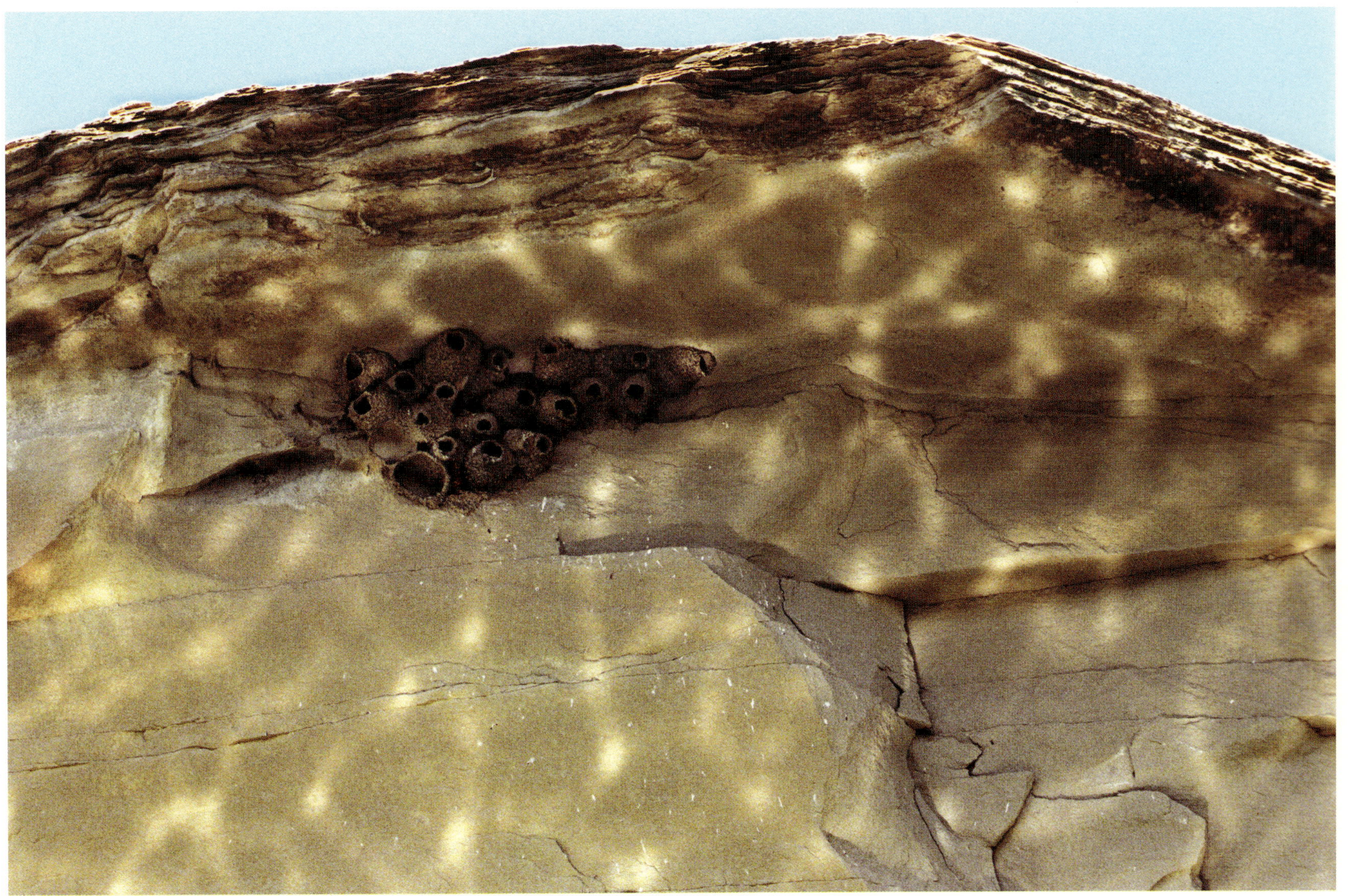

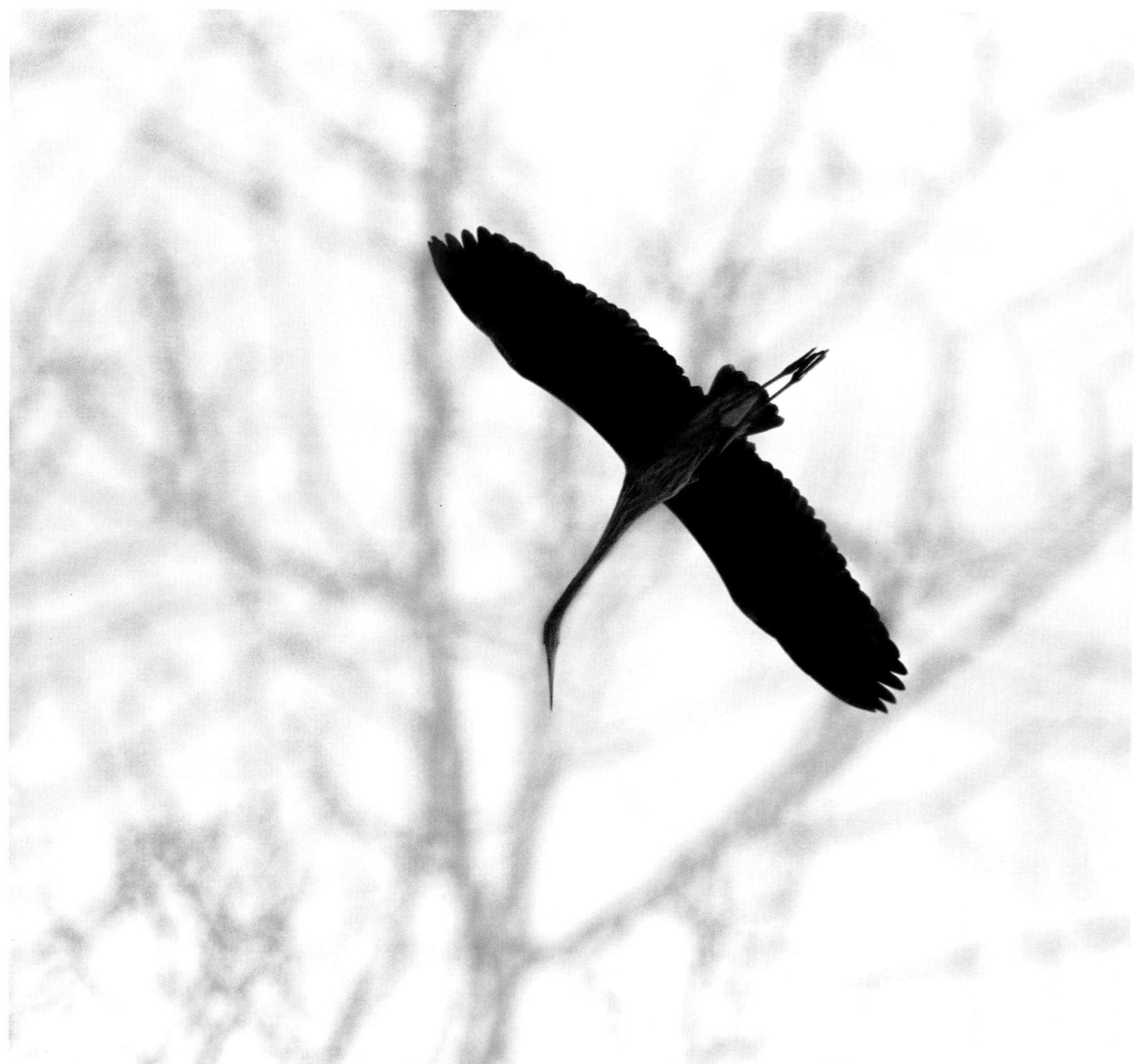

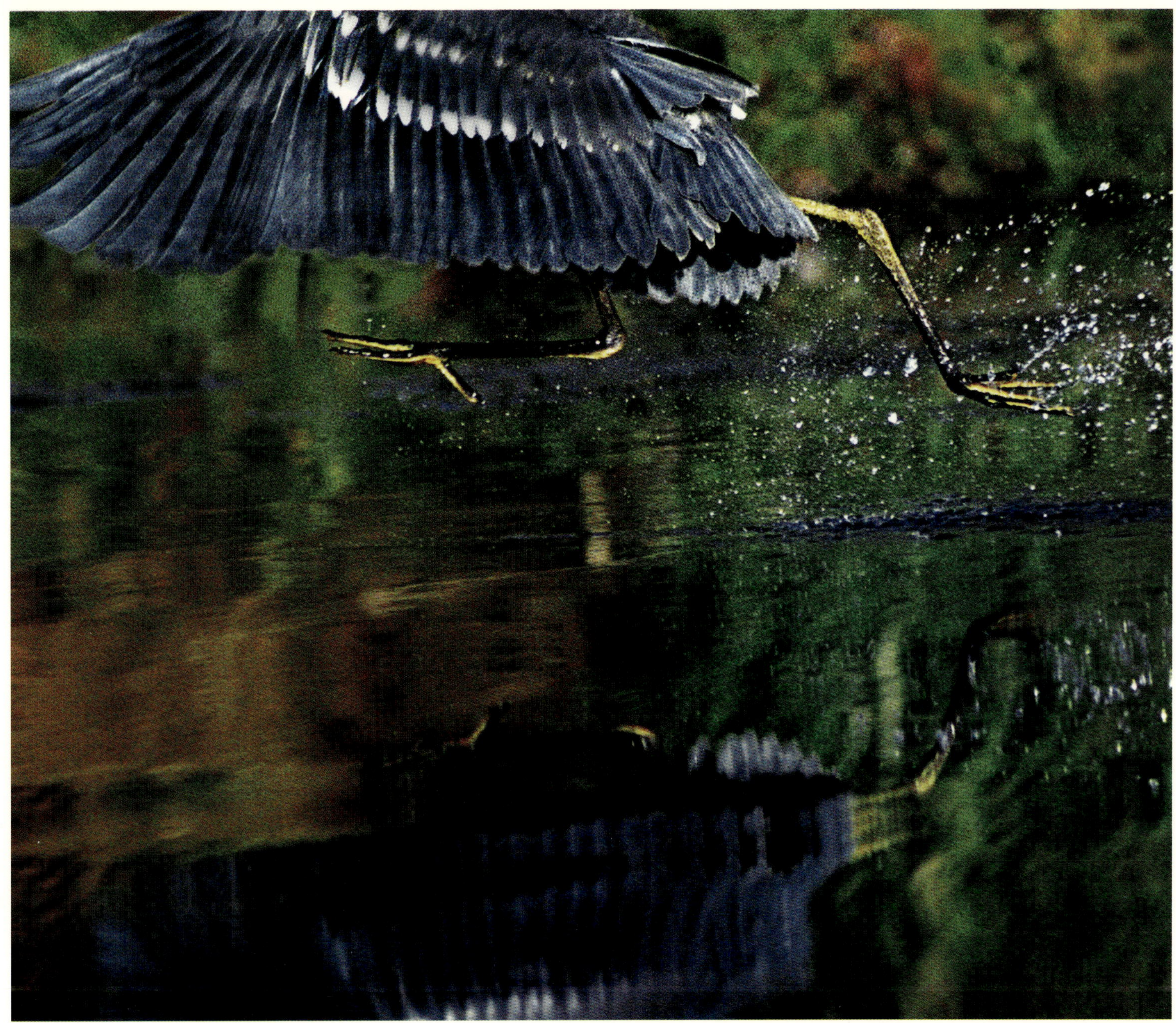

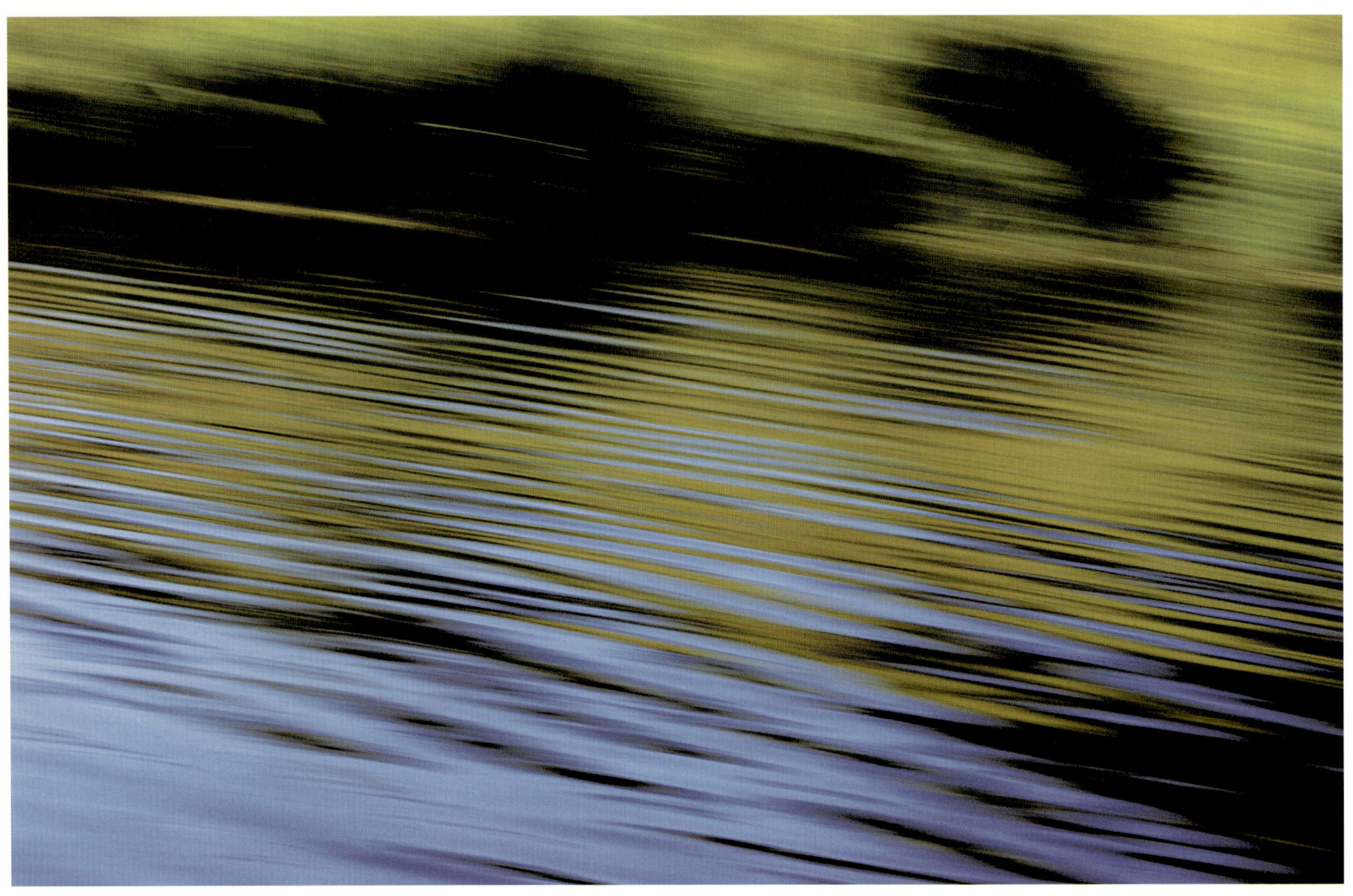

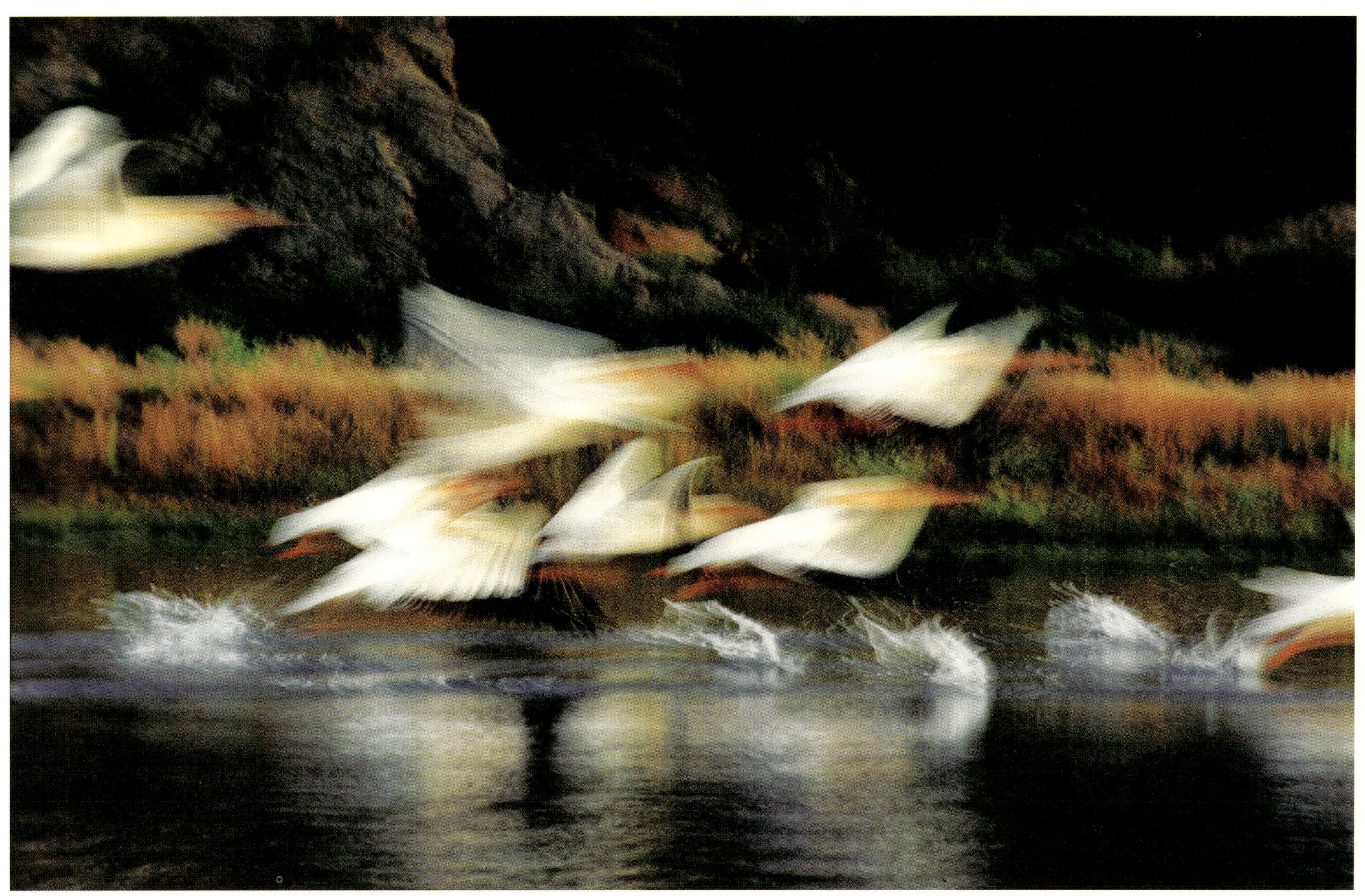

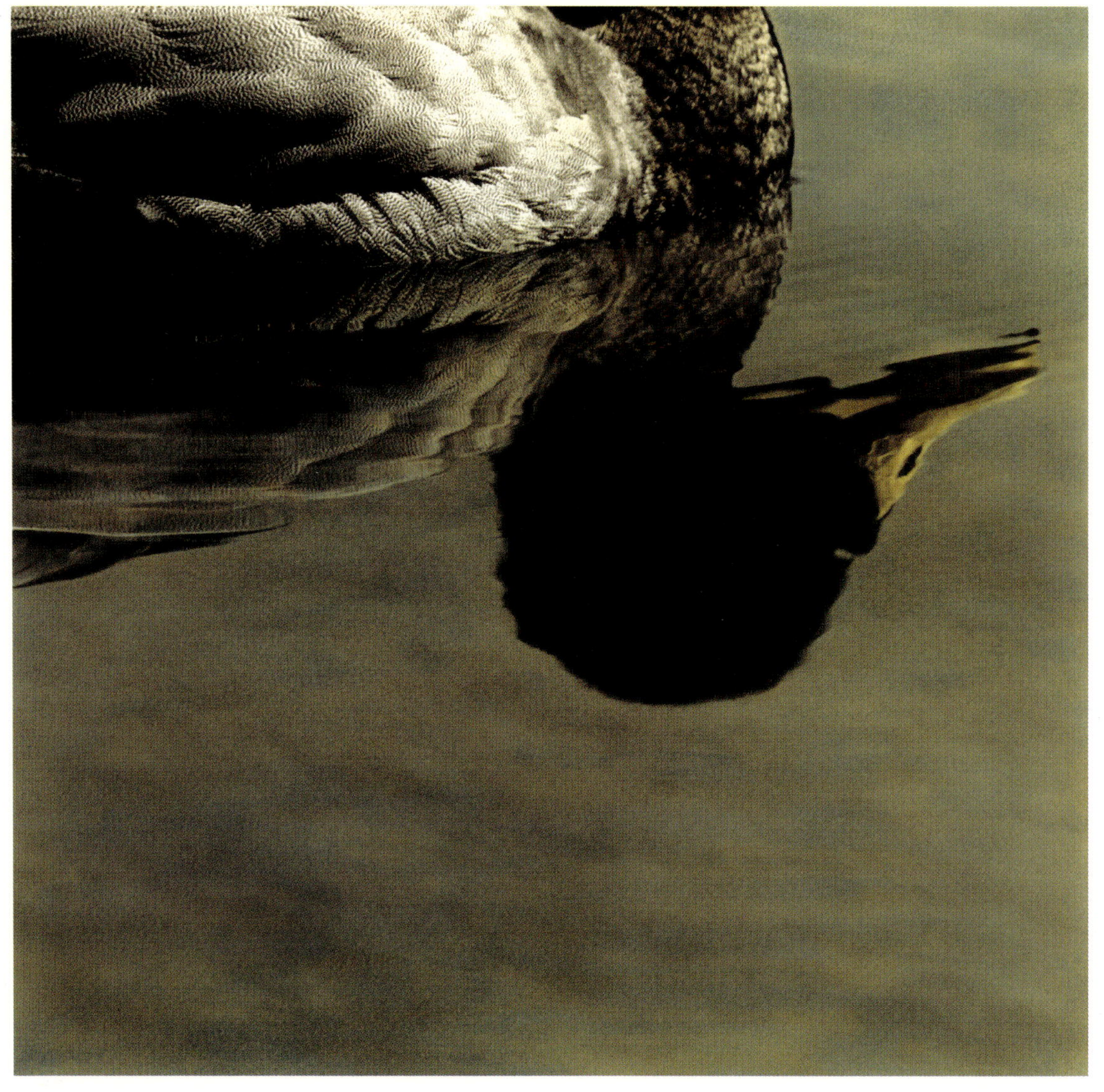

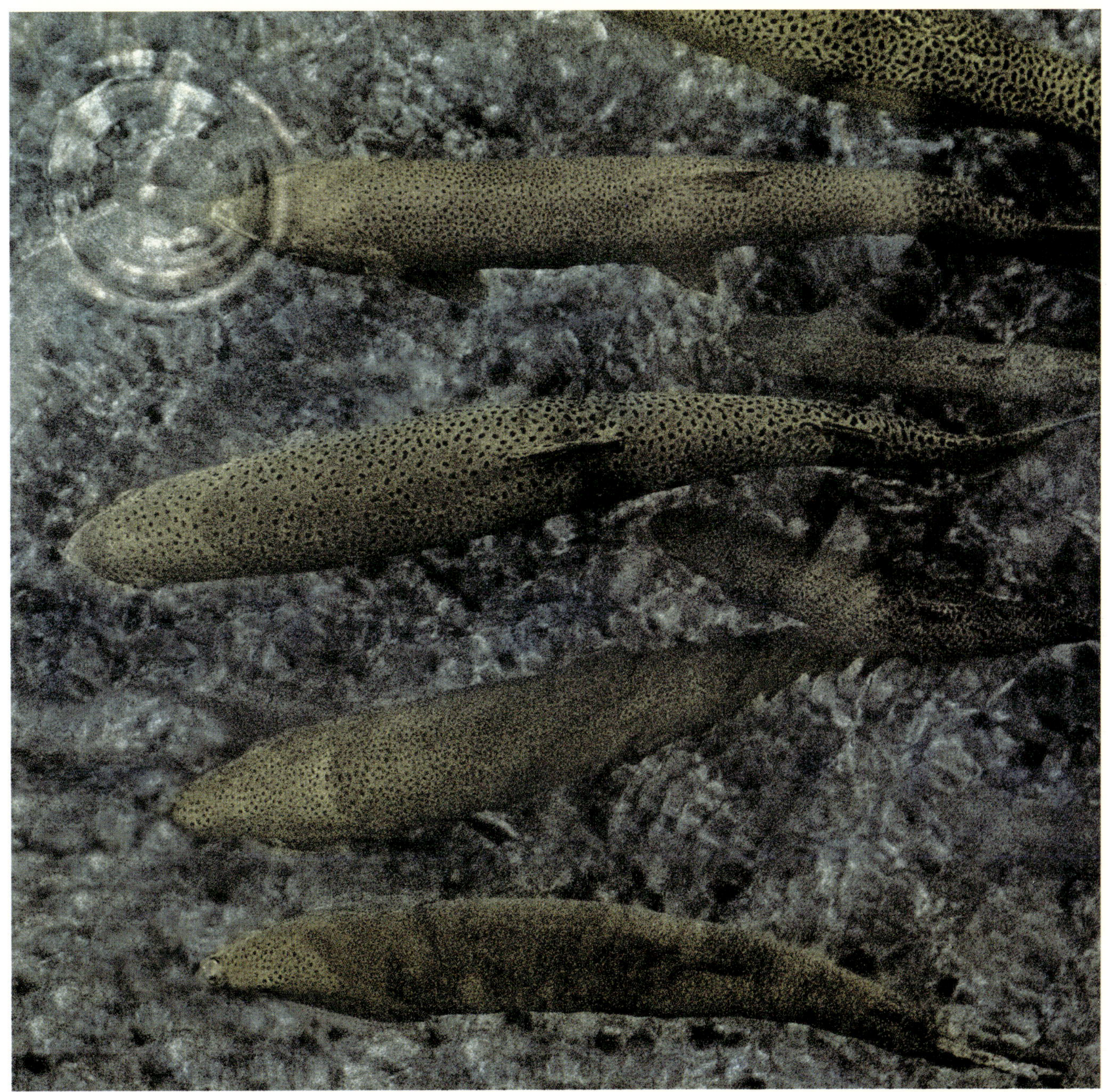

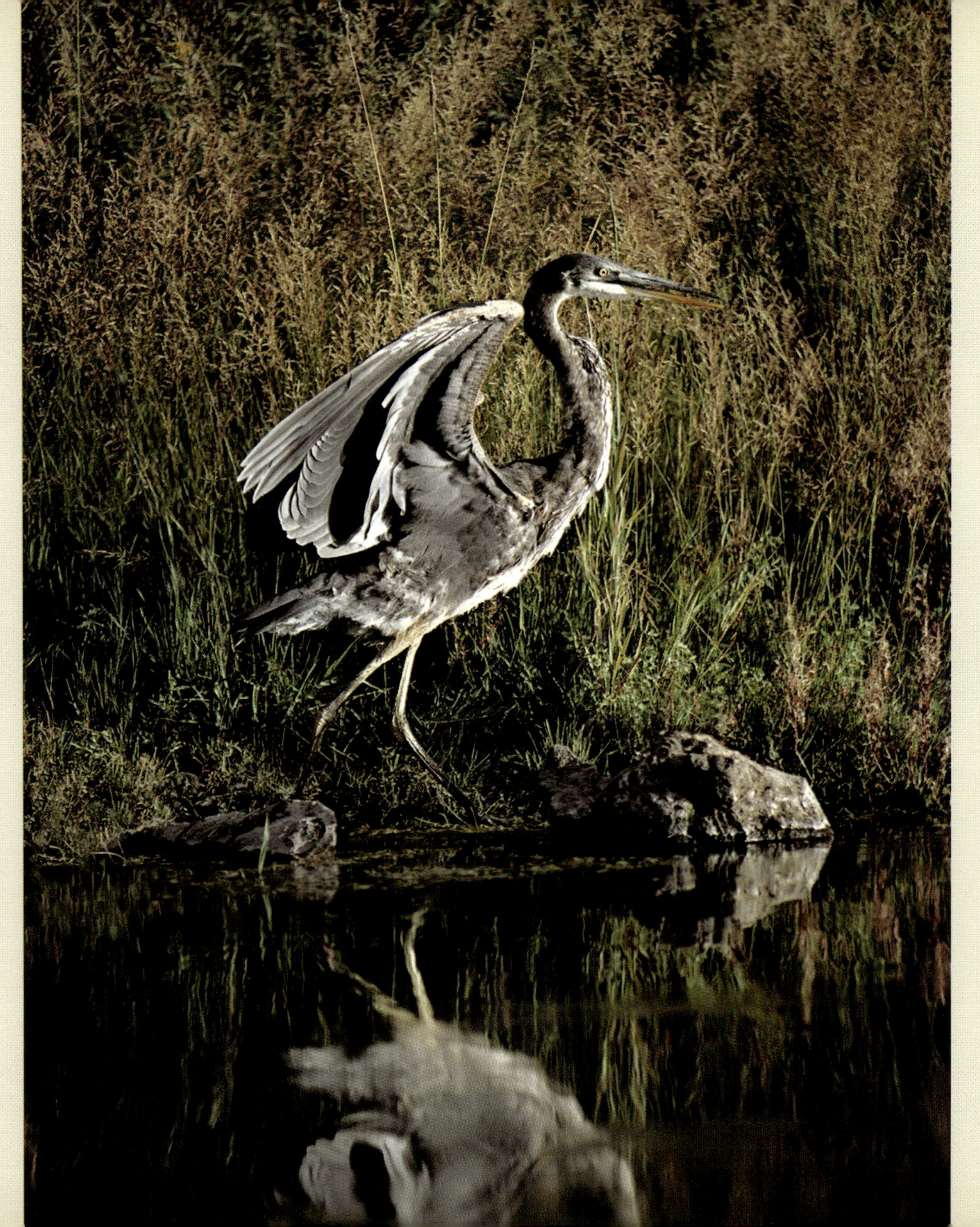

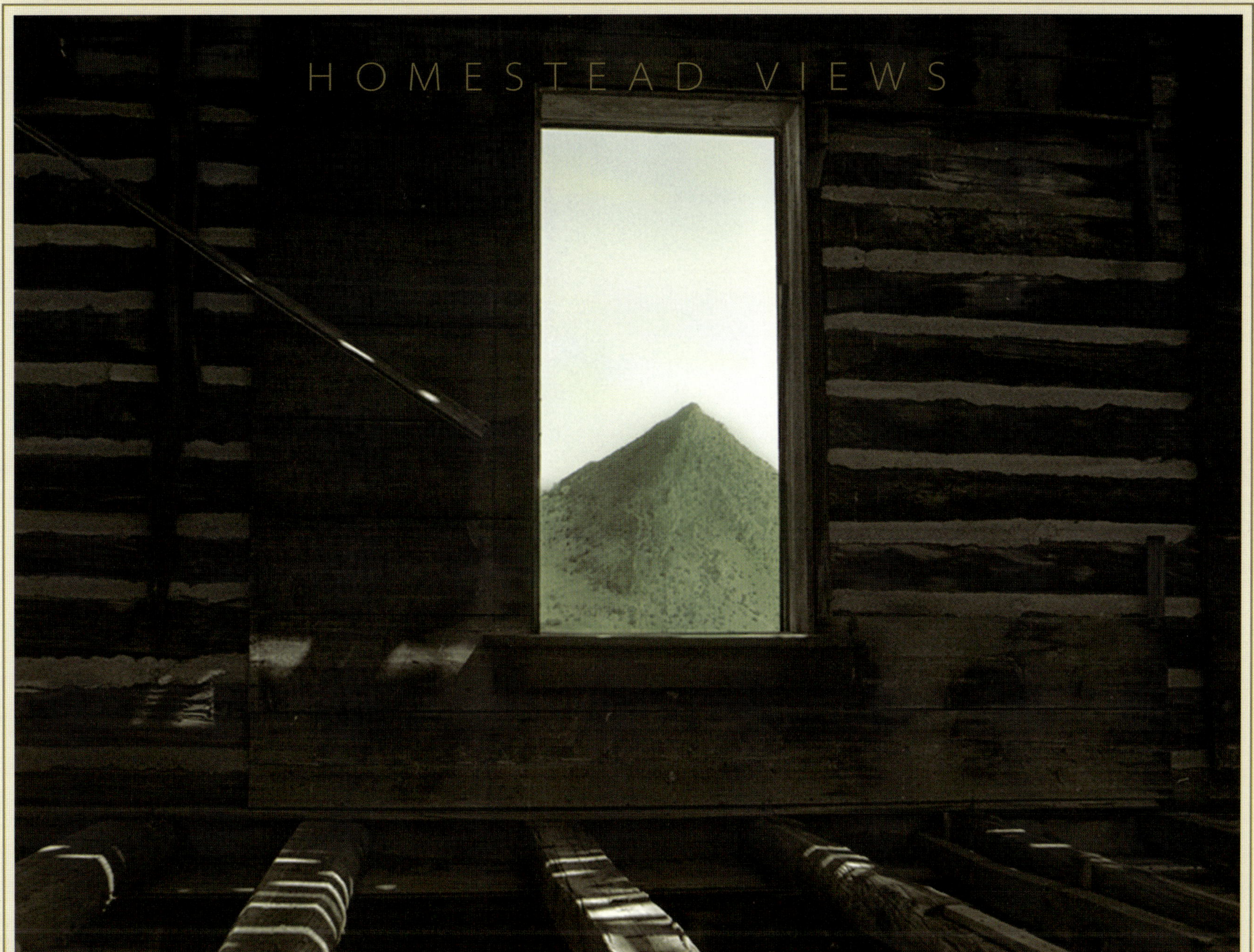
HOMESTEAD VIEWS

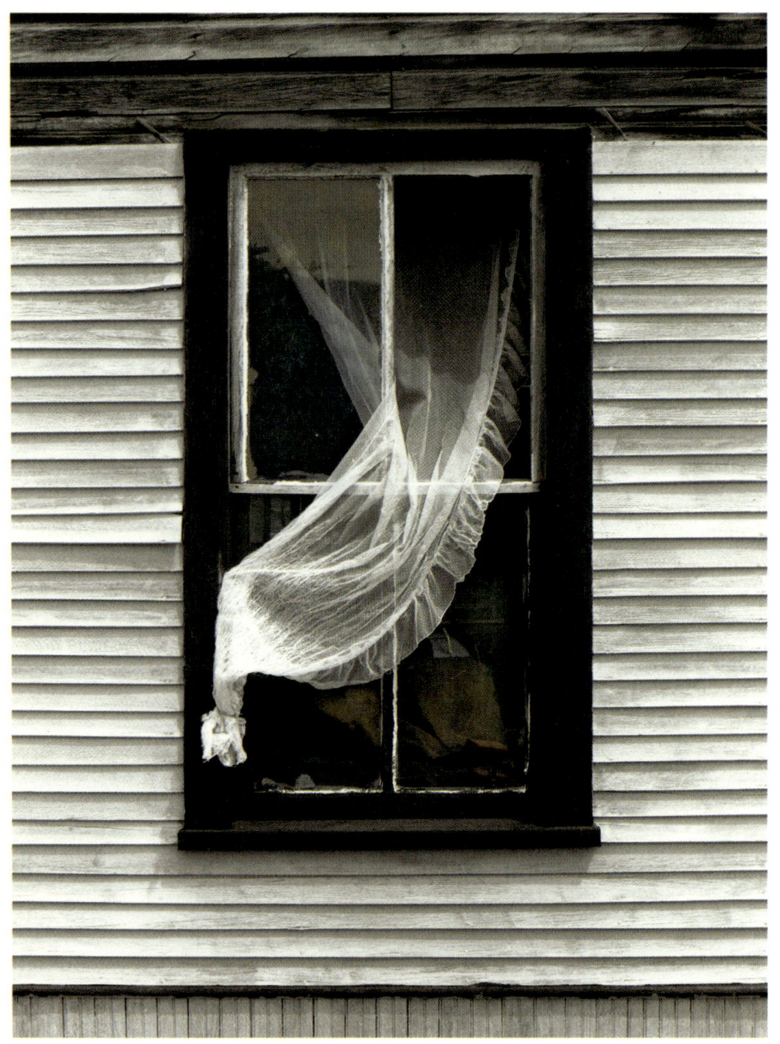

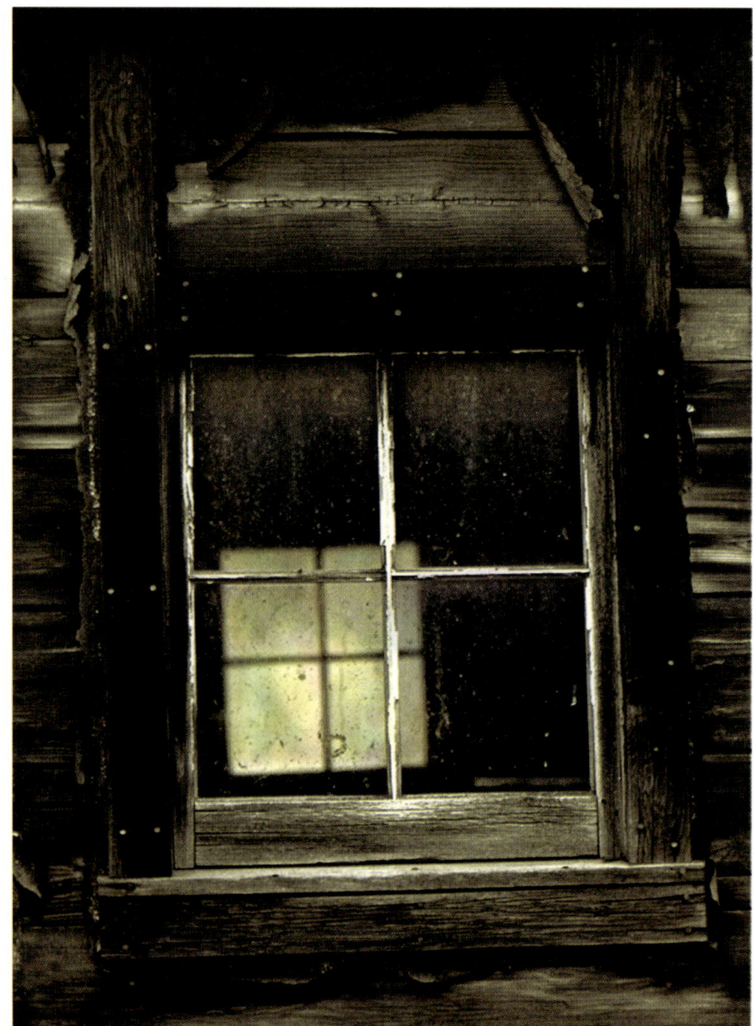

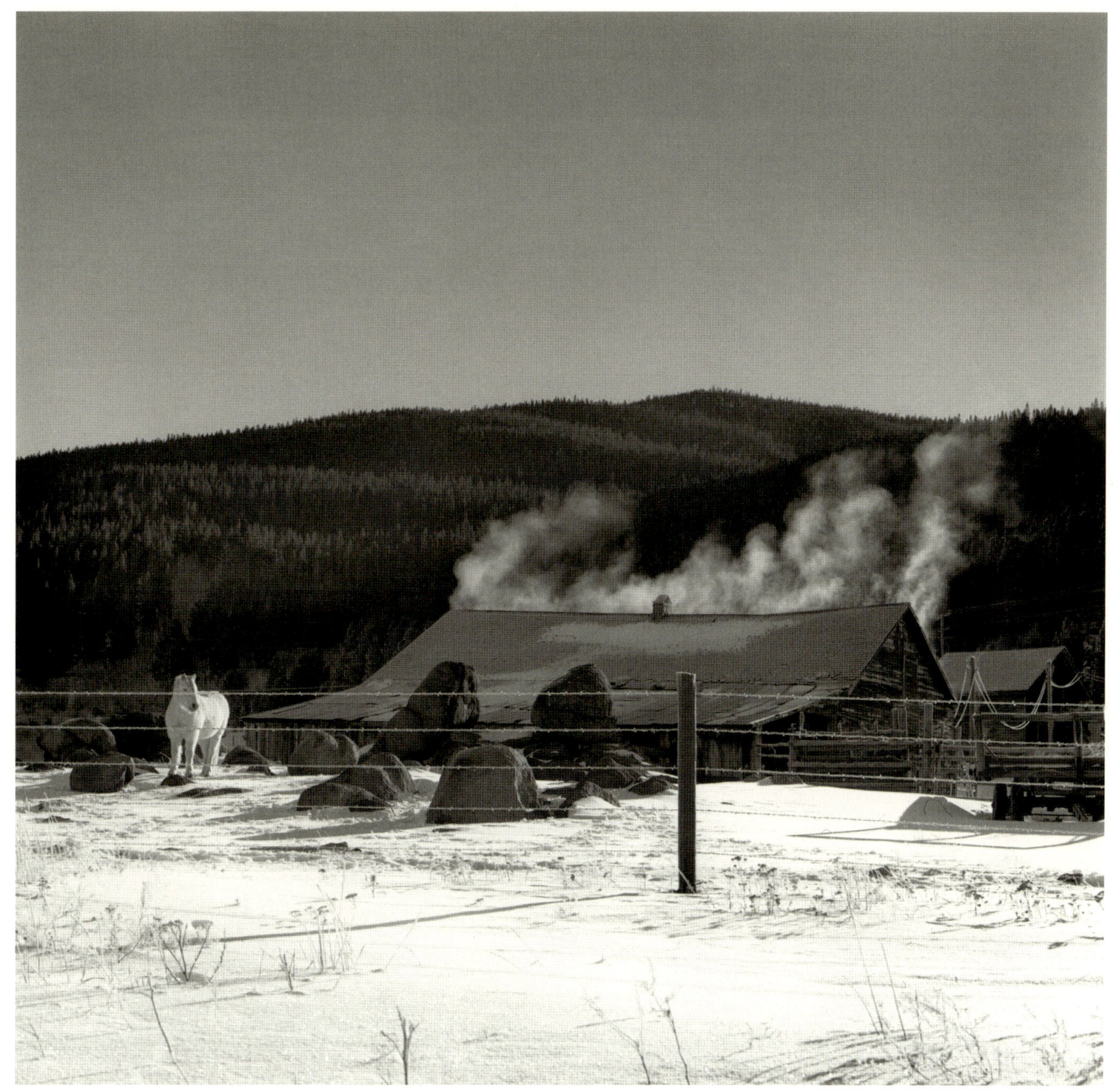

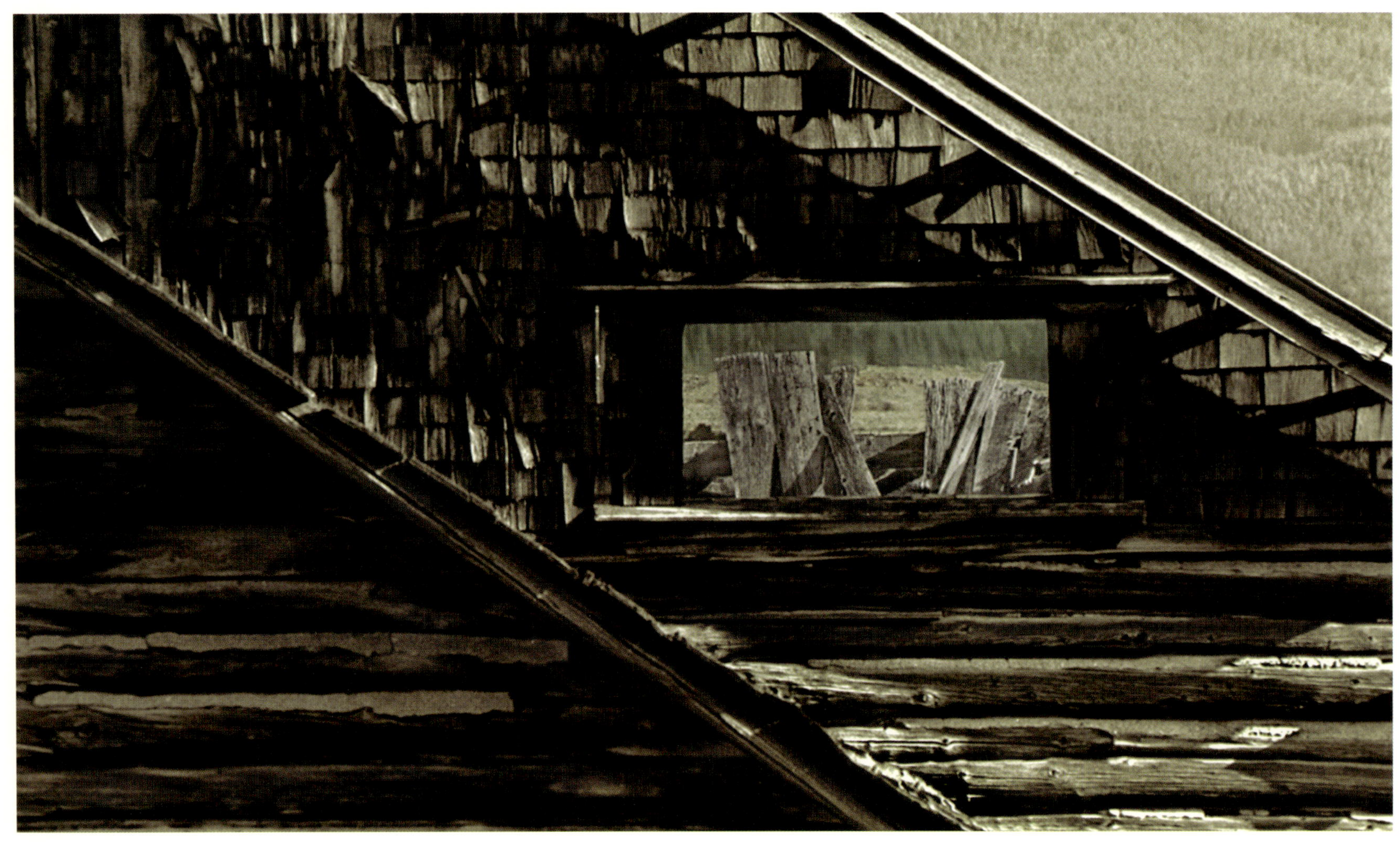

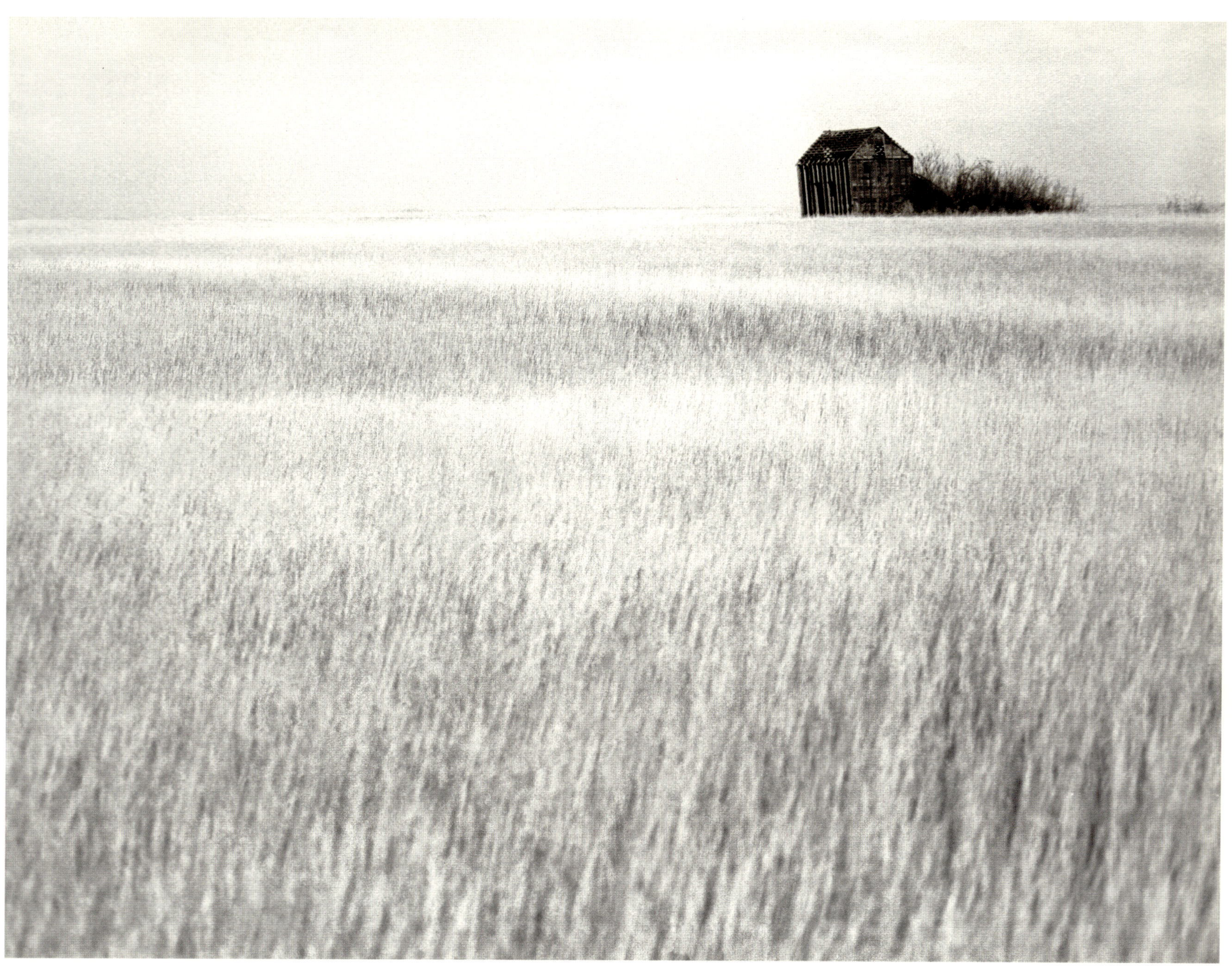

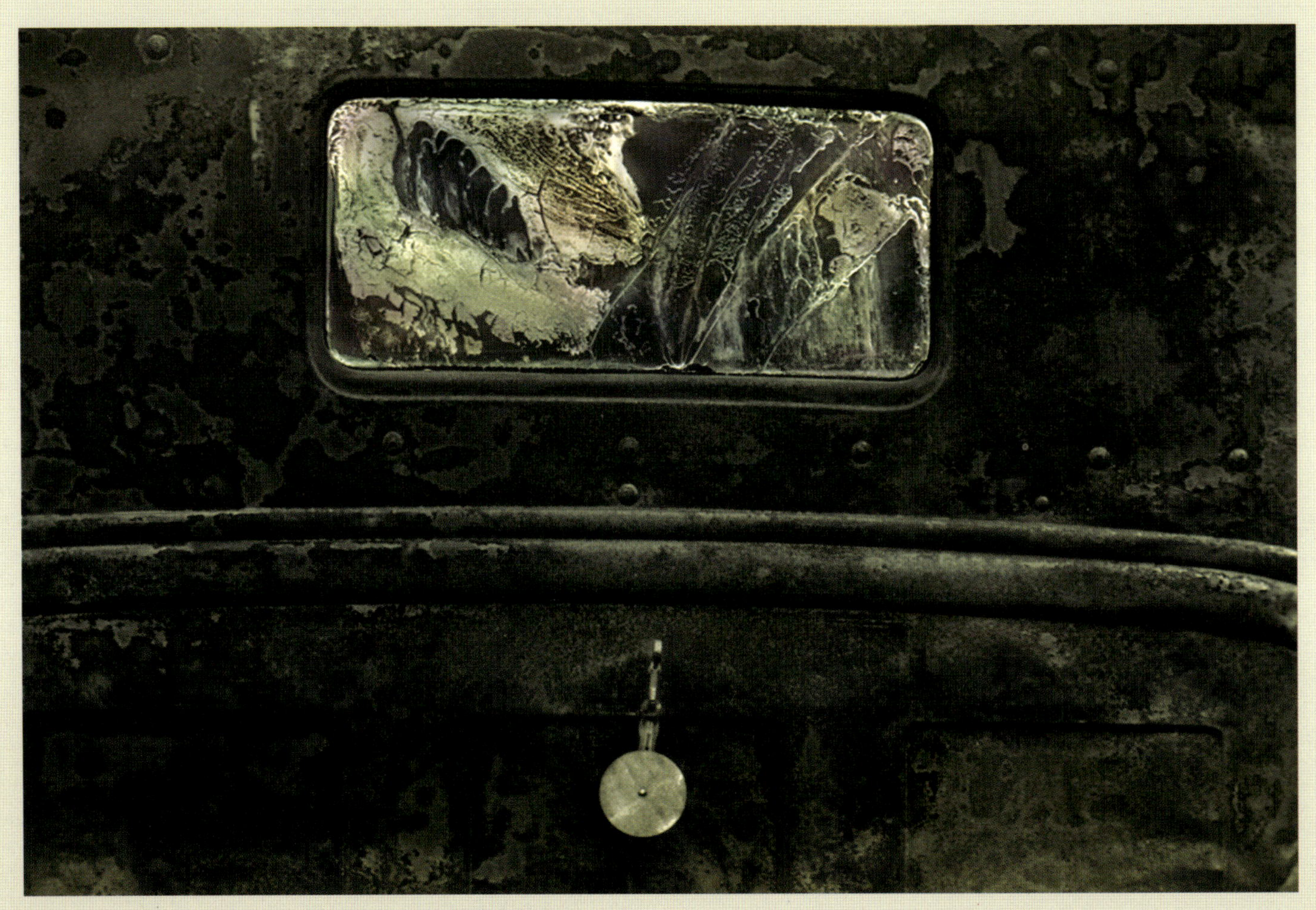

SHEARING

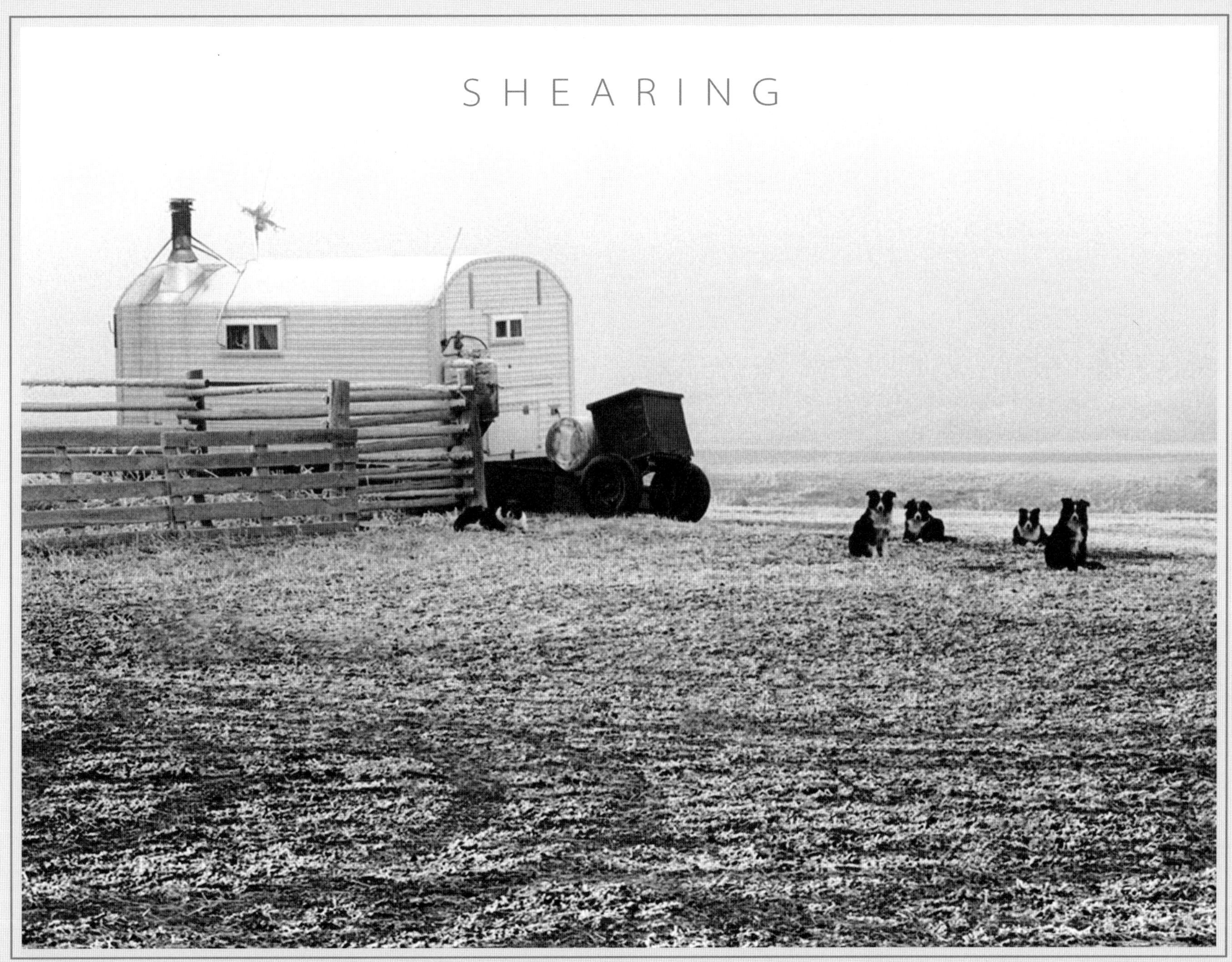

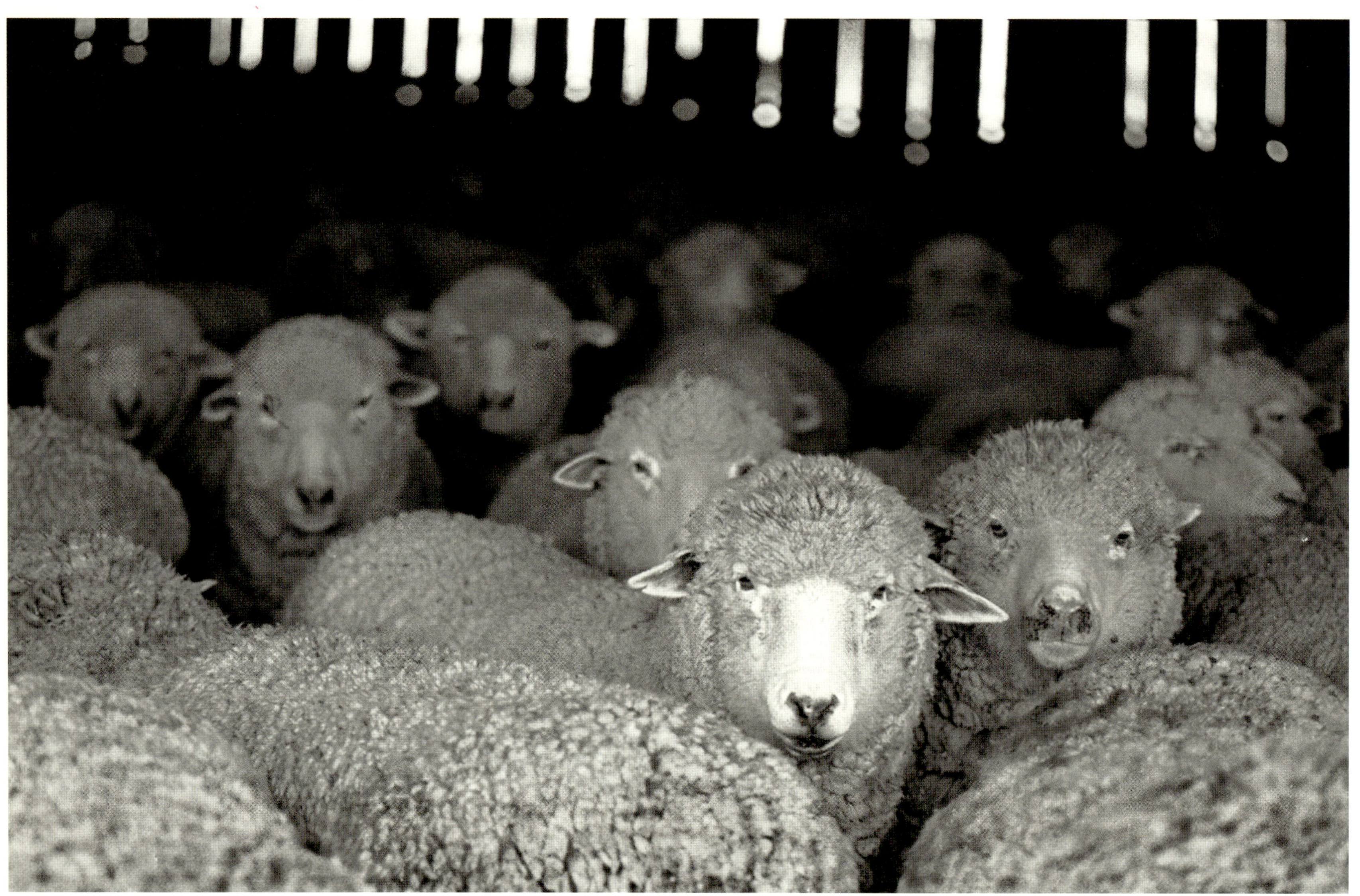

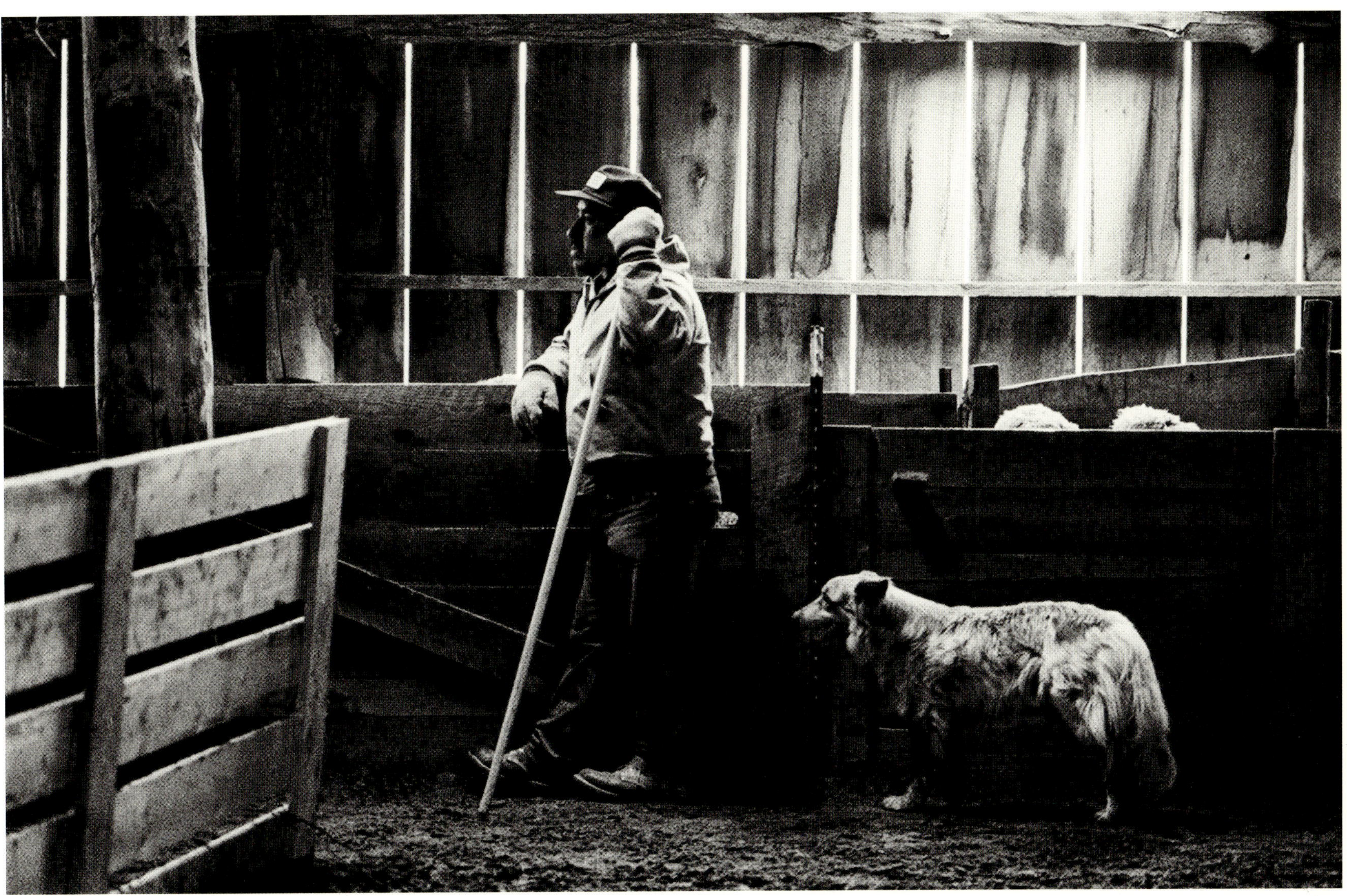

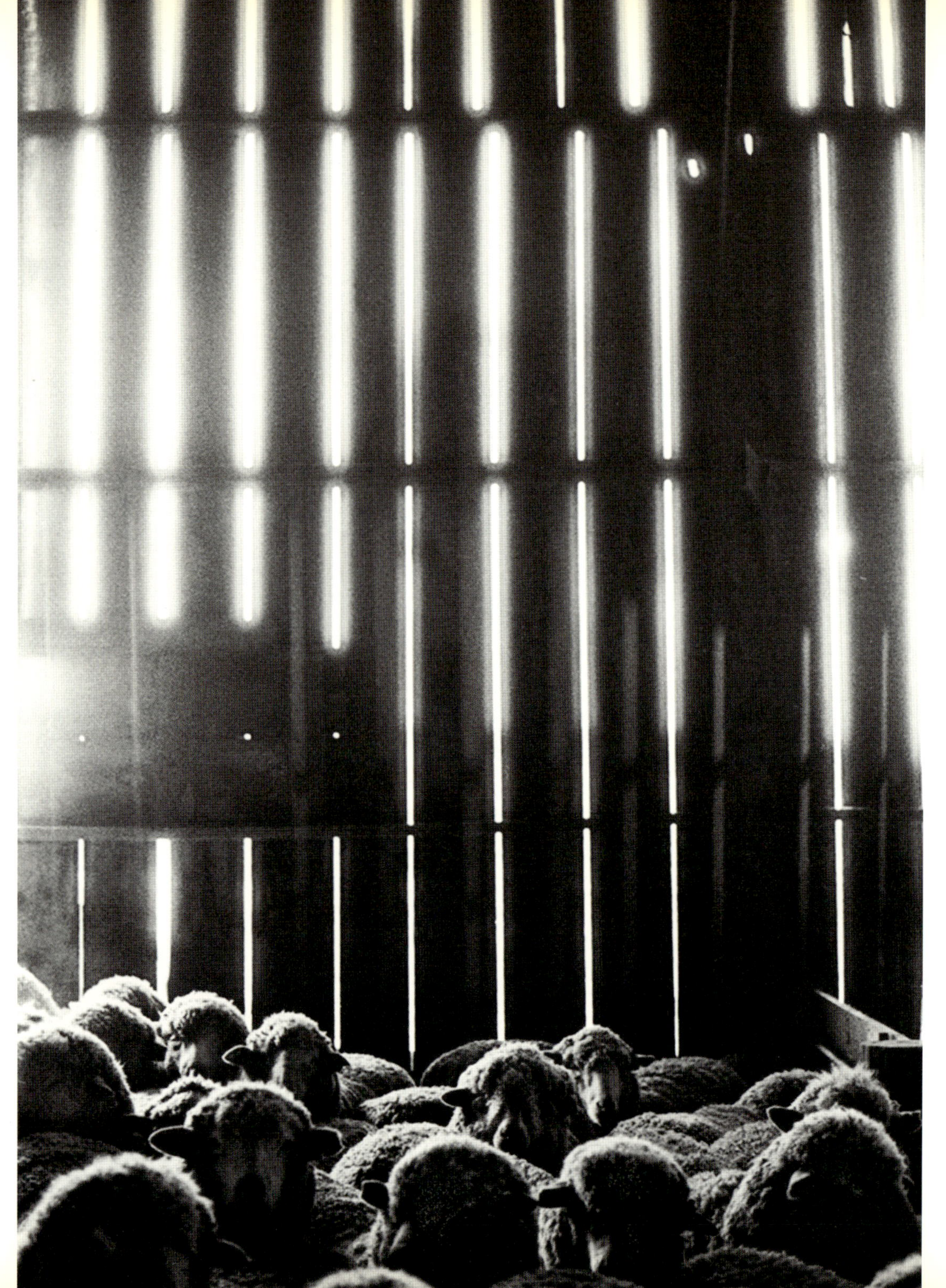

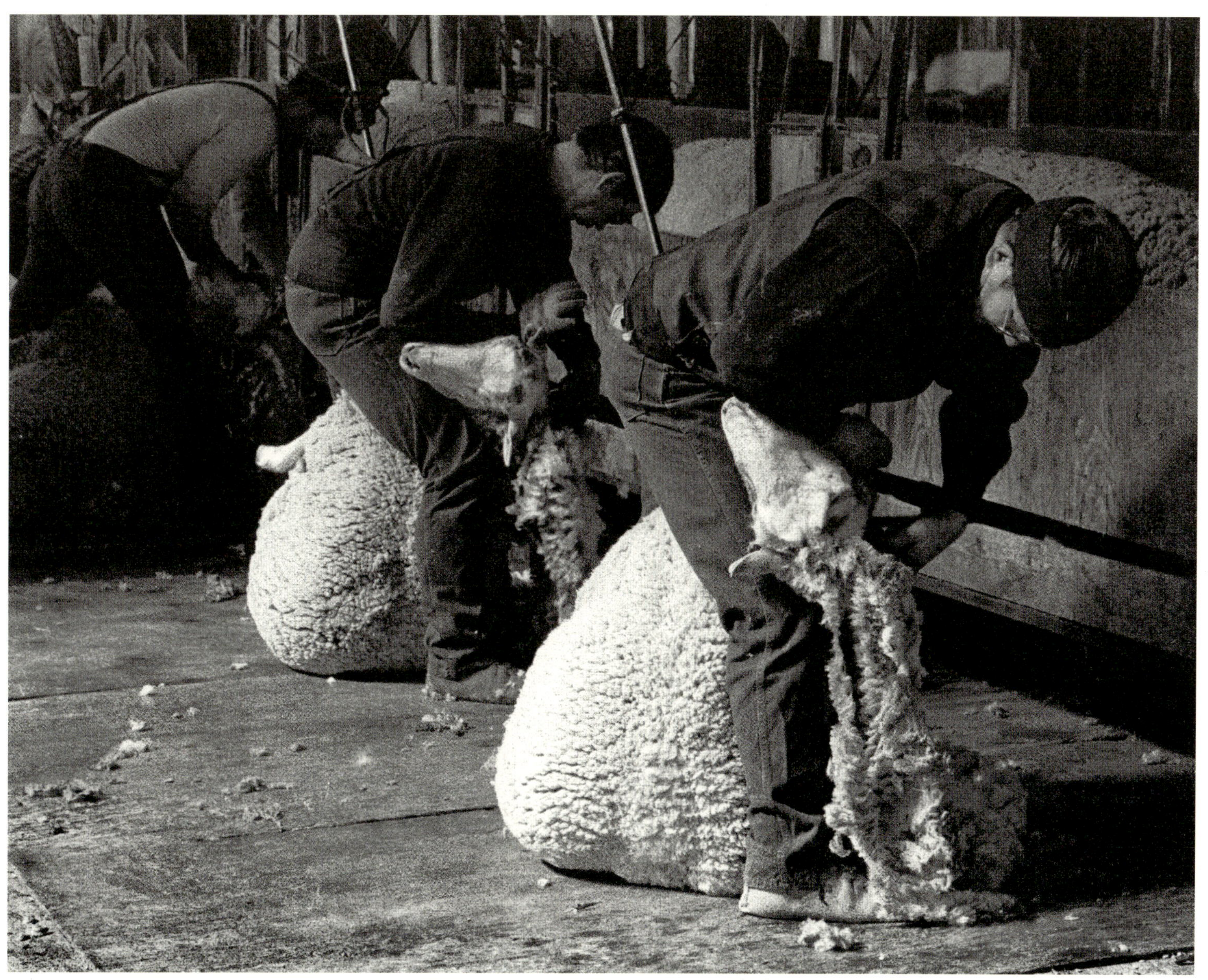

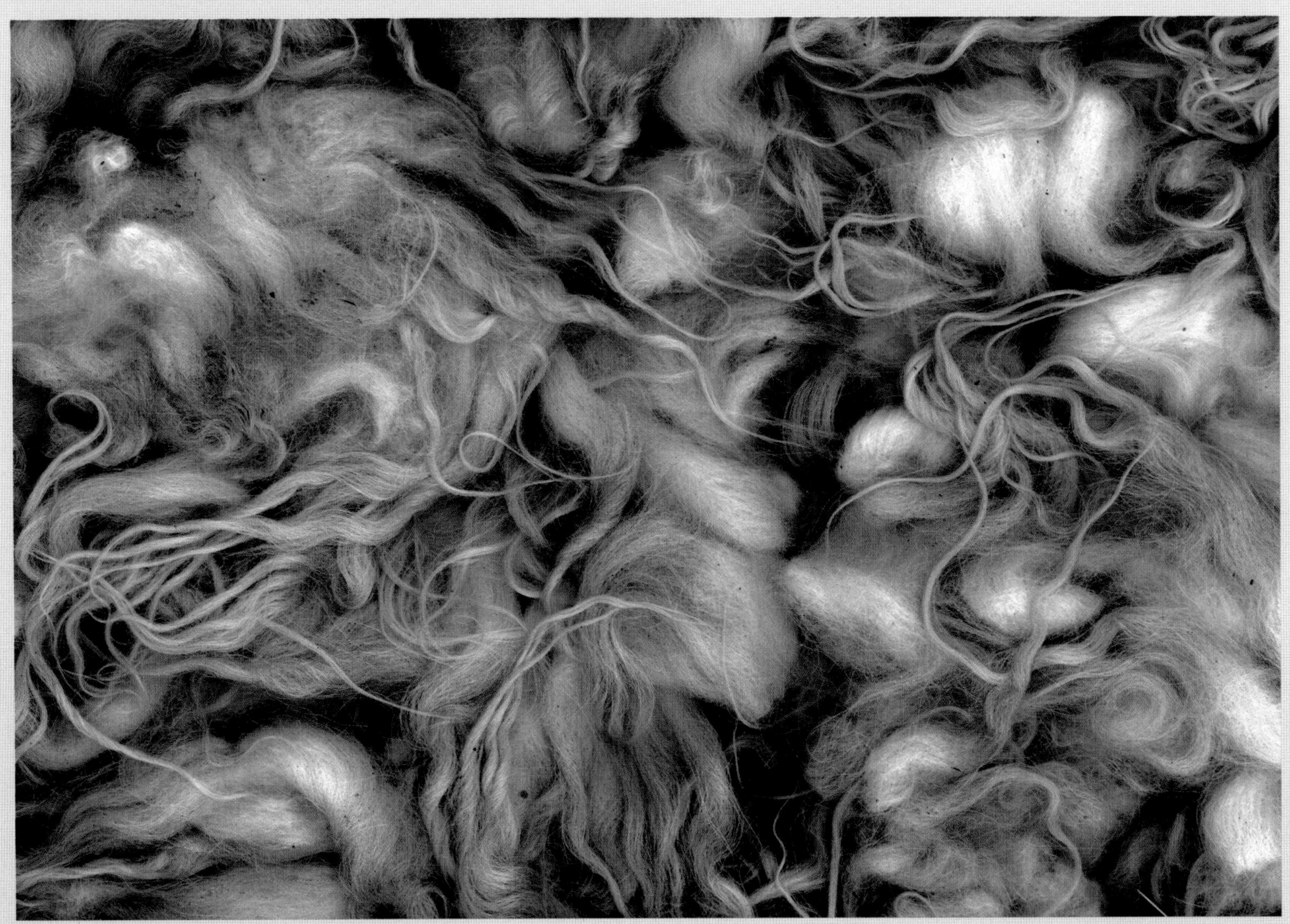

RANCHING

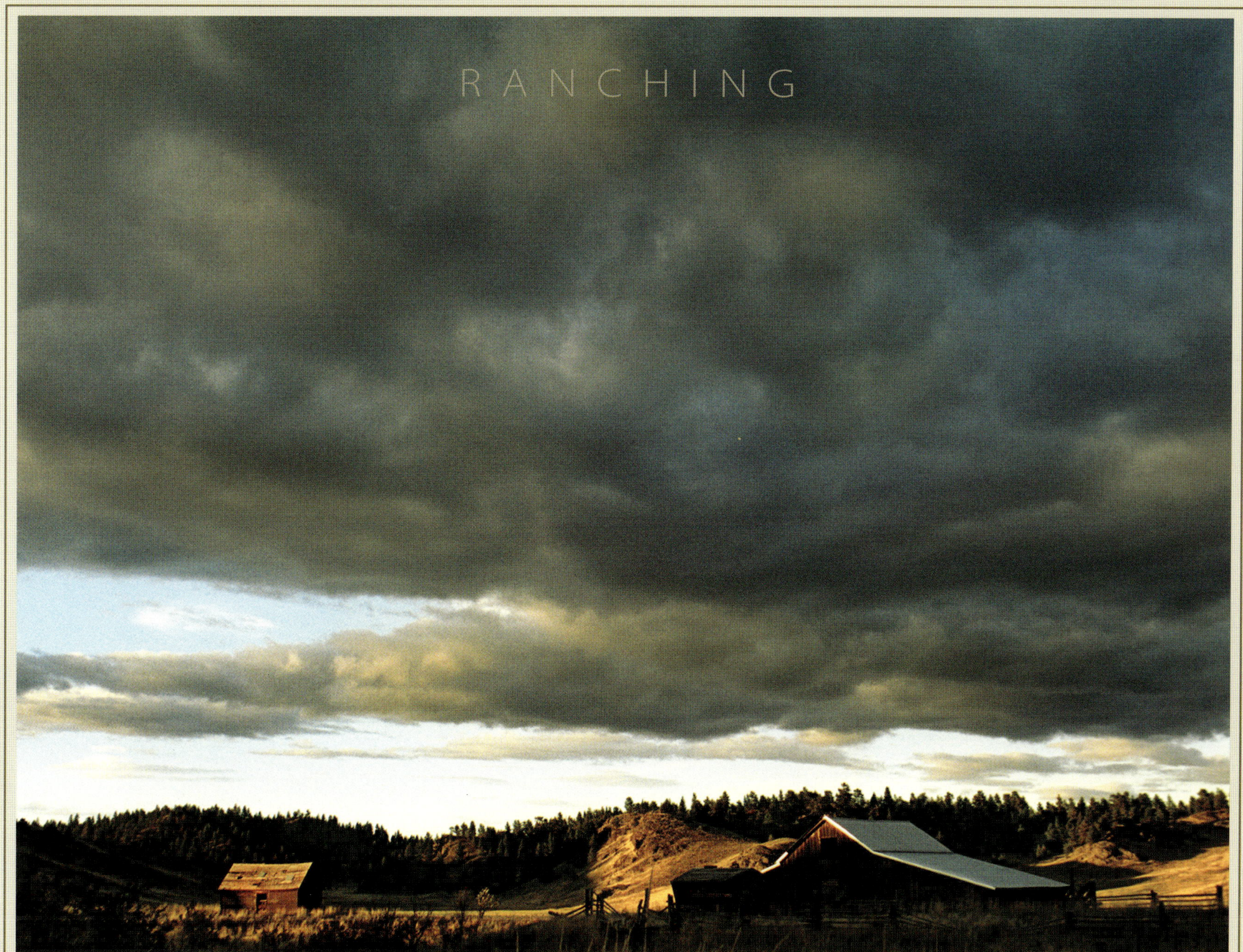

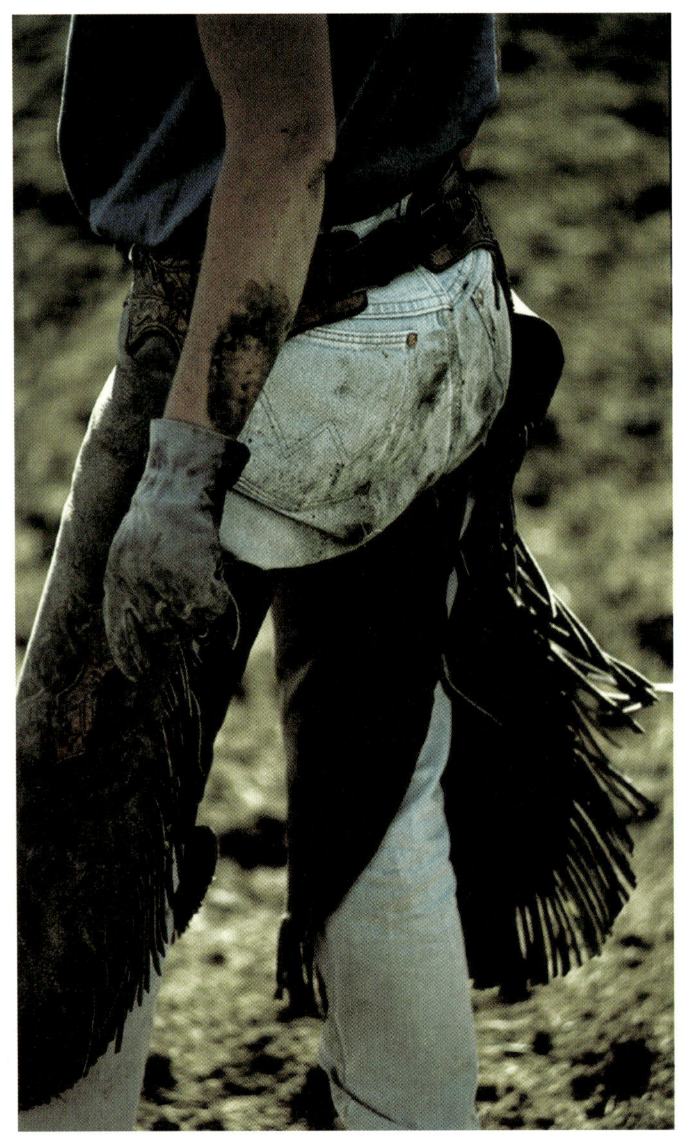

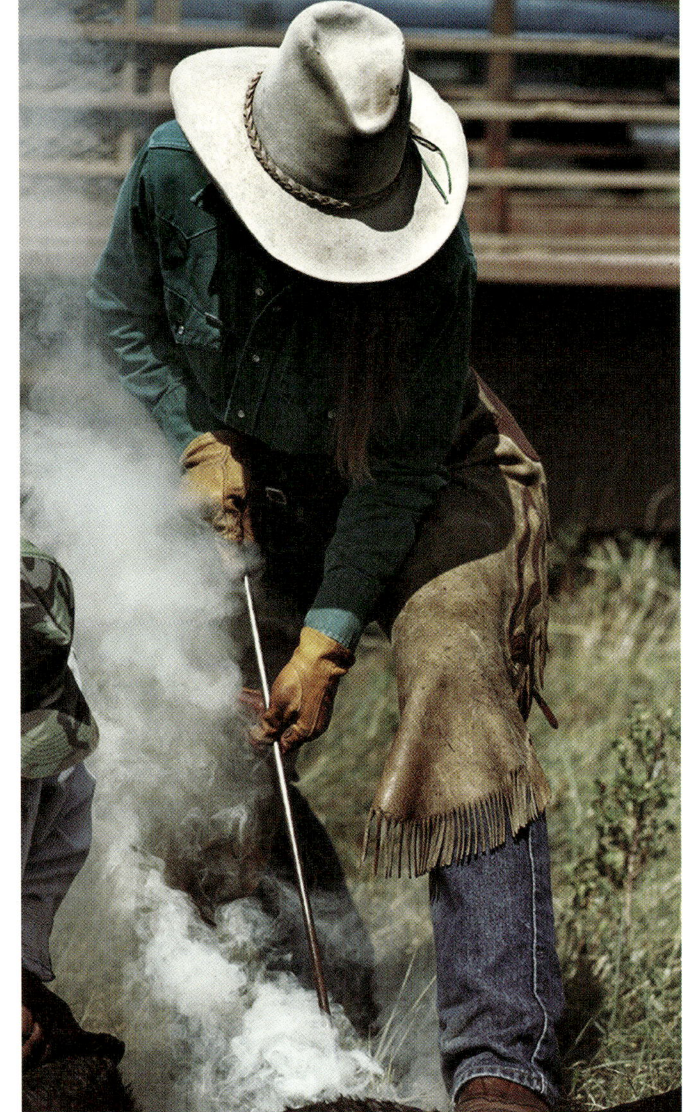

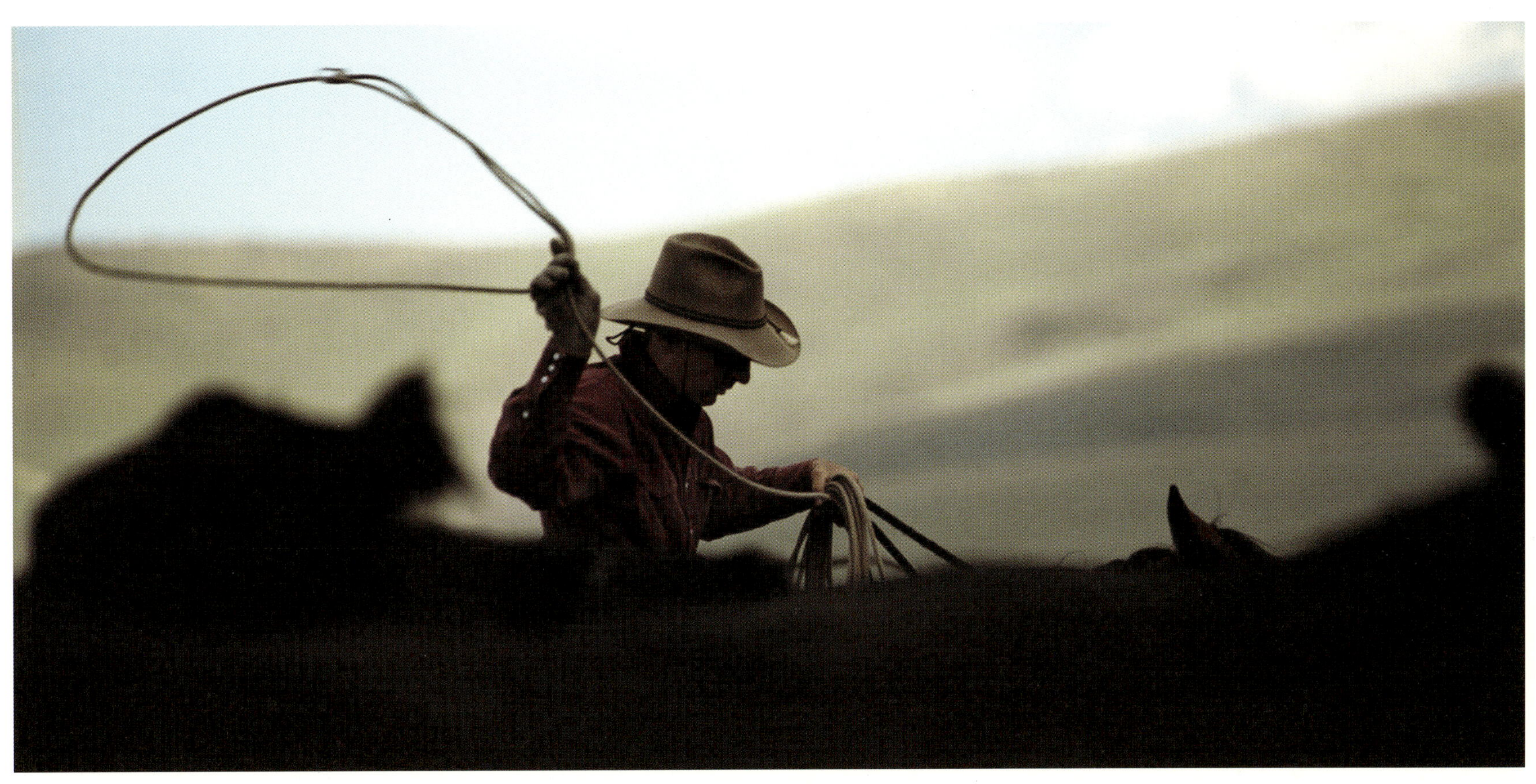

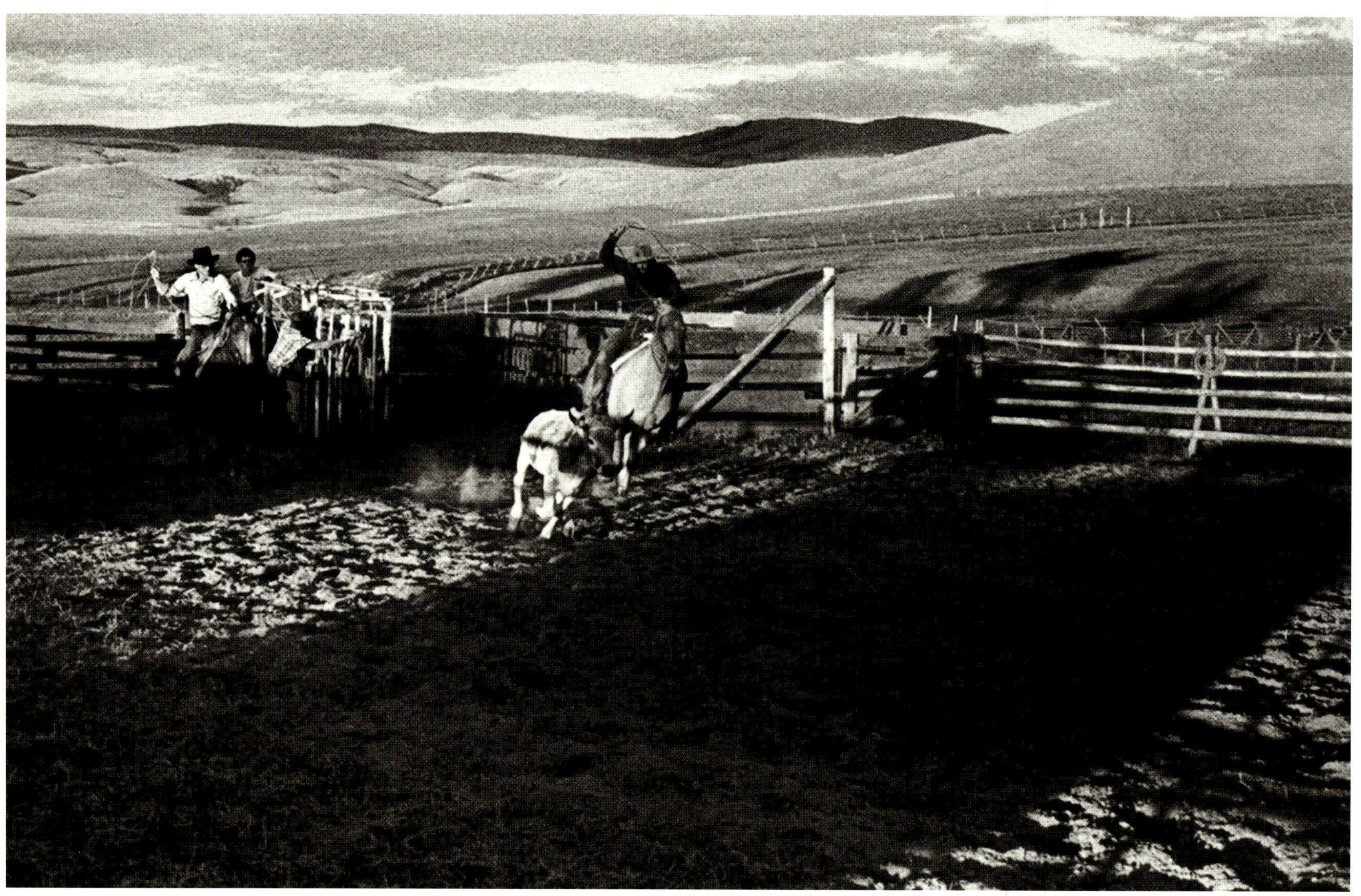

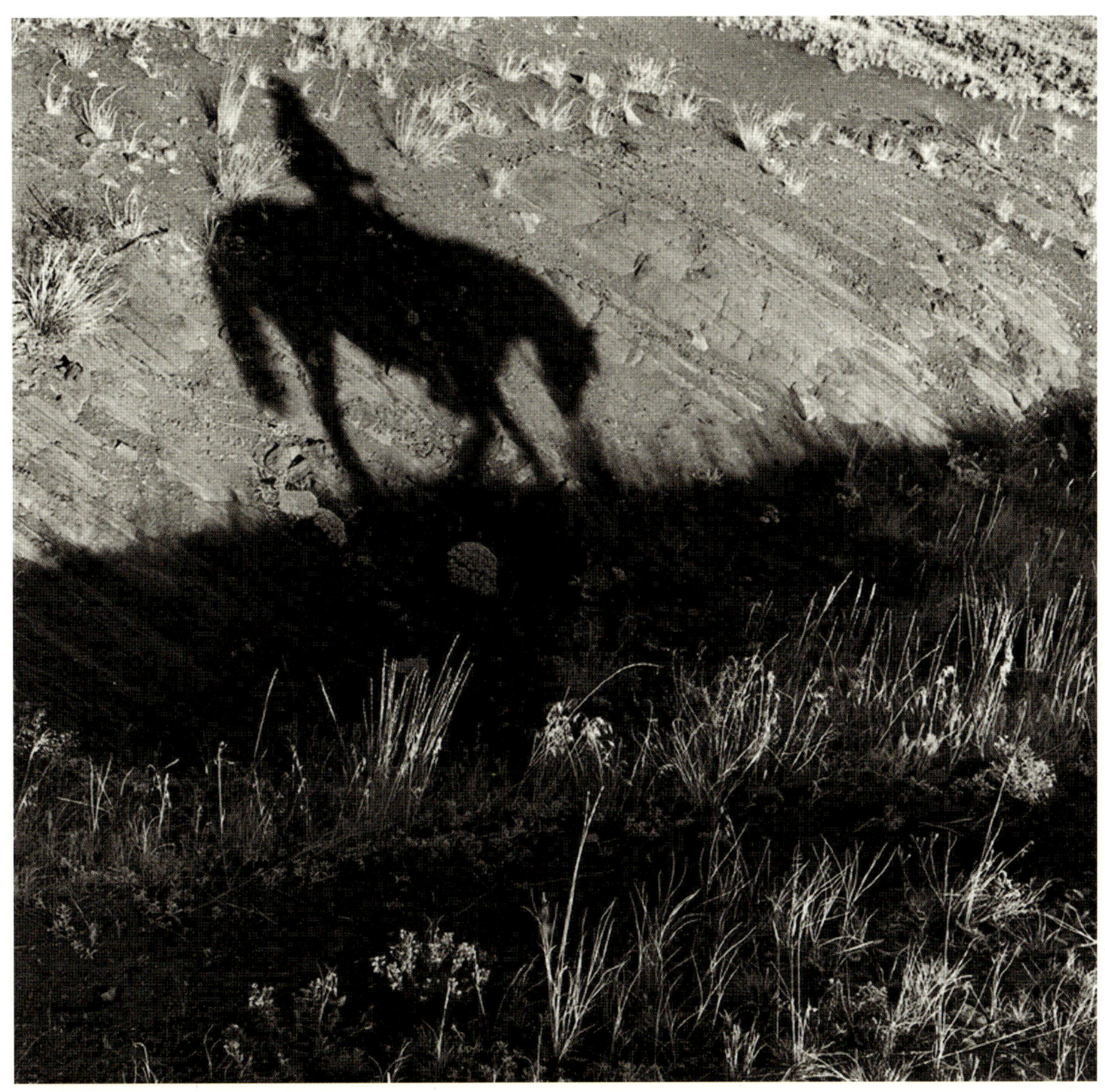

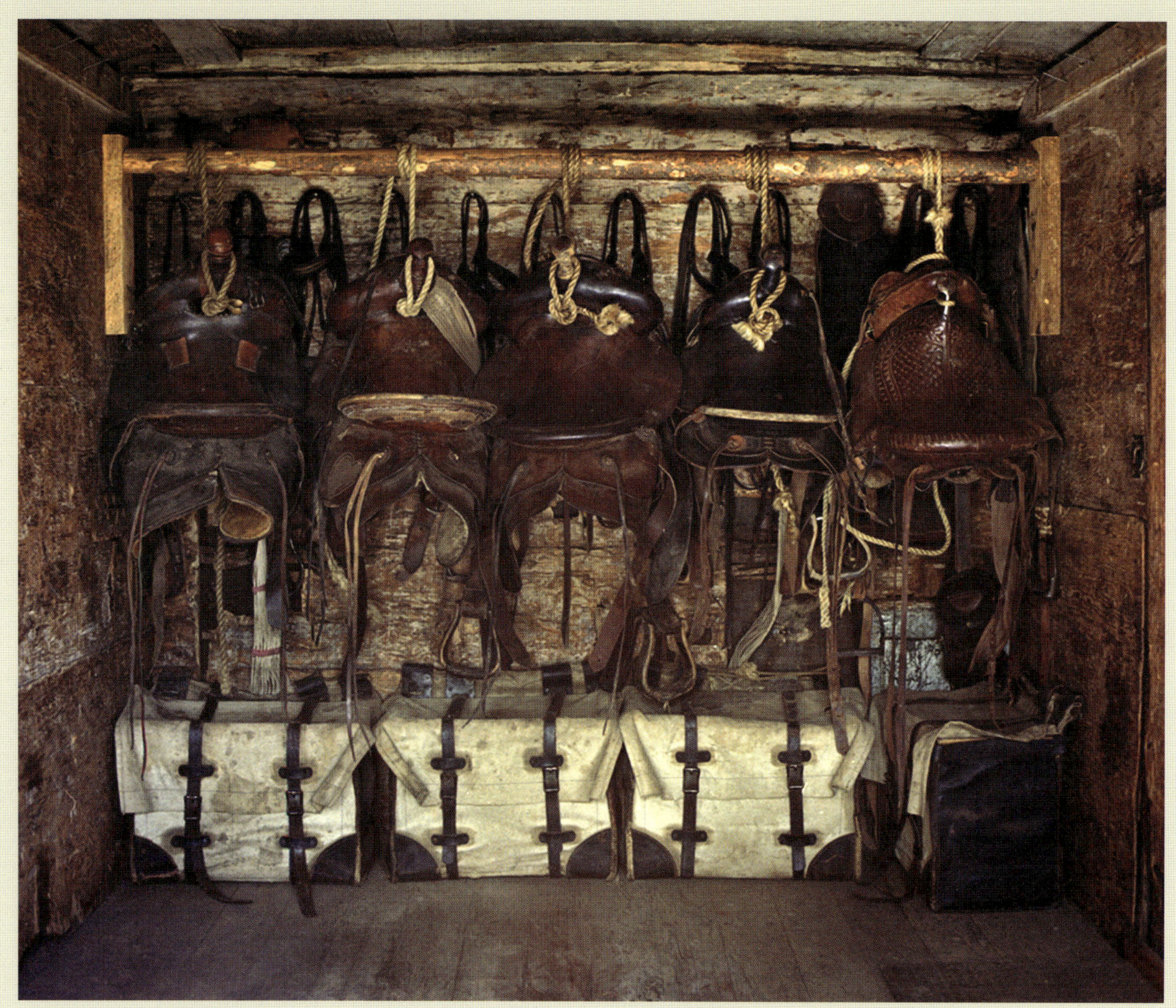

NATIVE AMERICANS

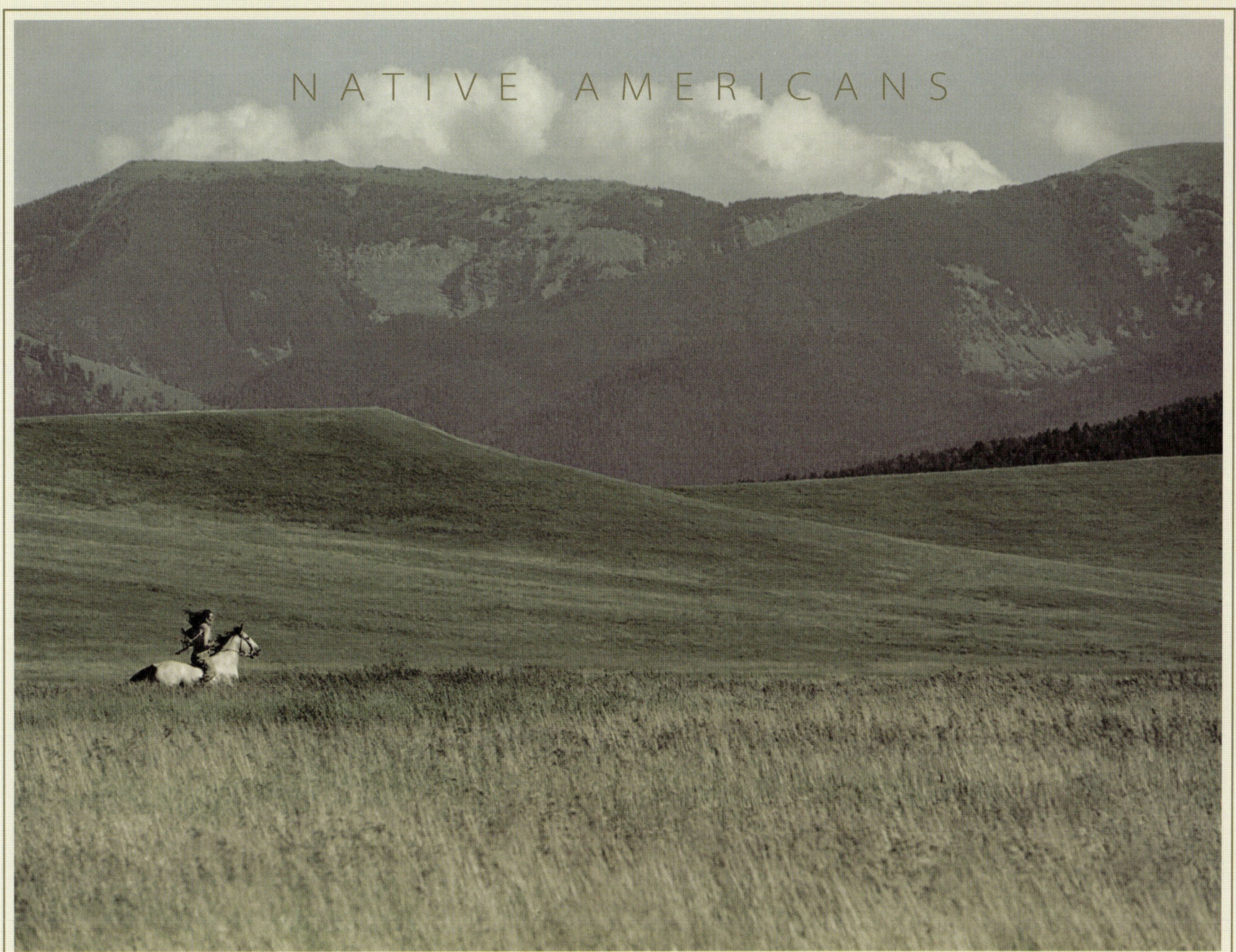

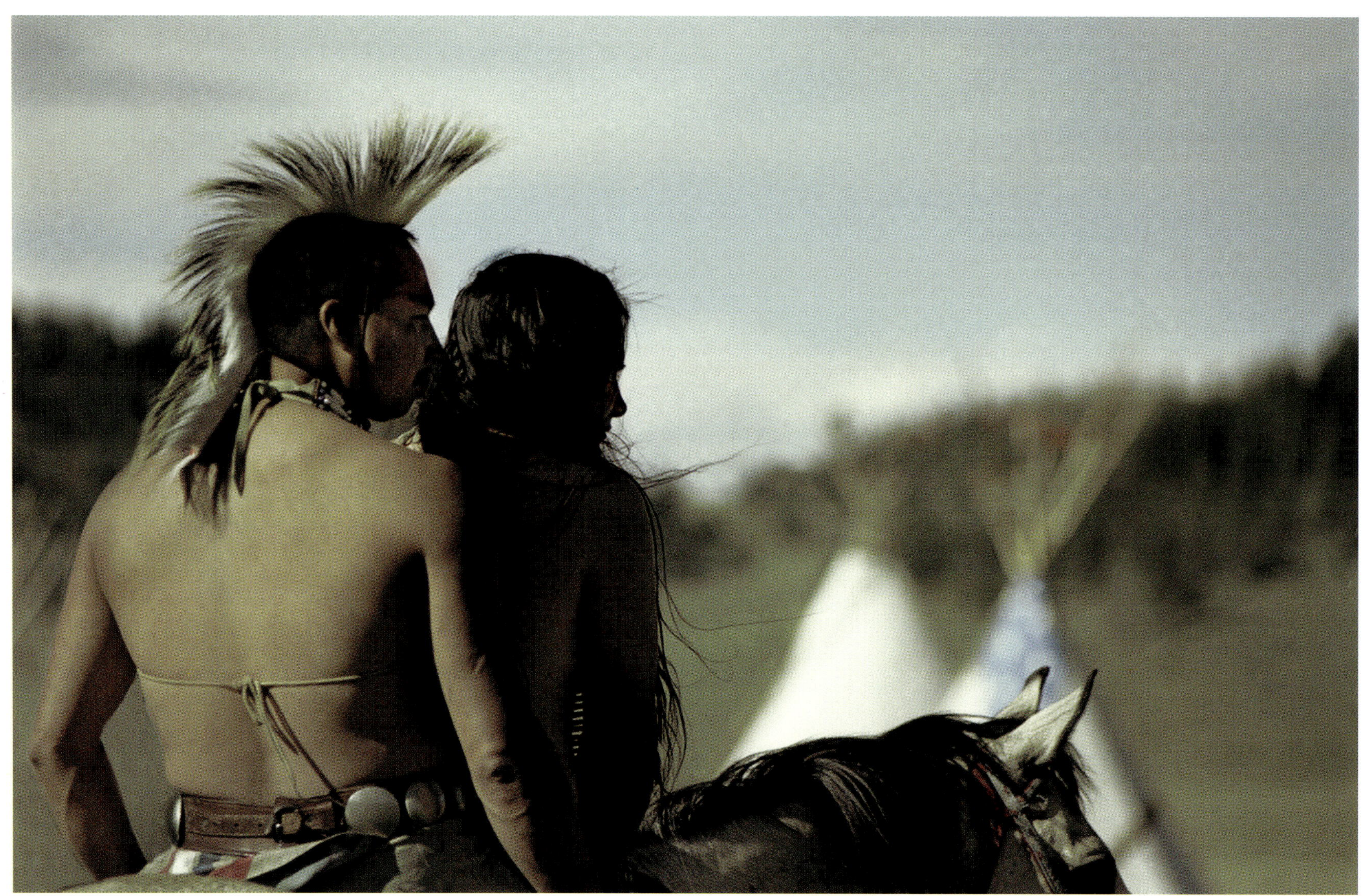

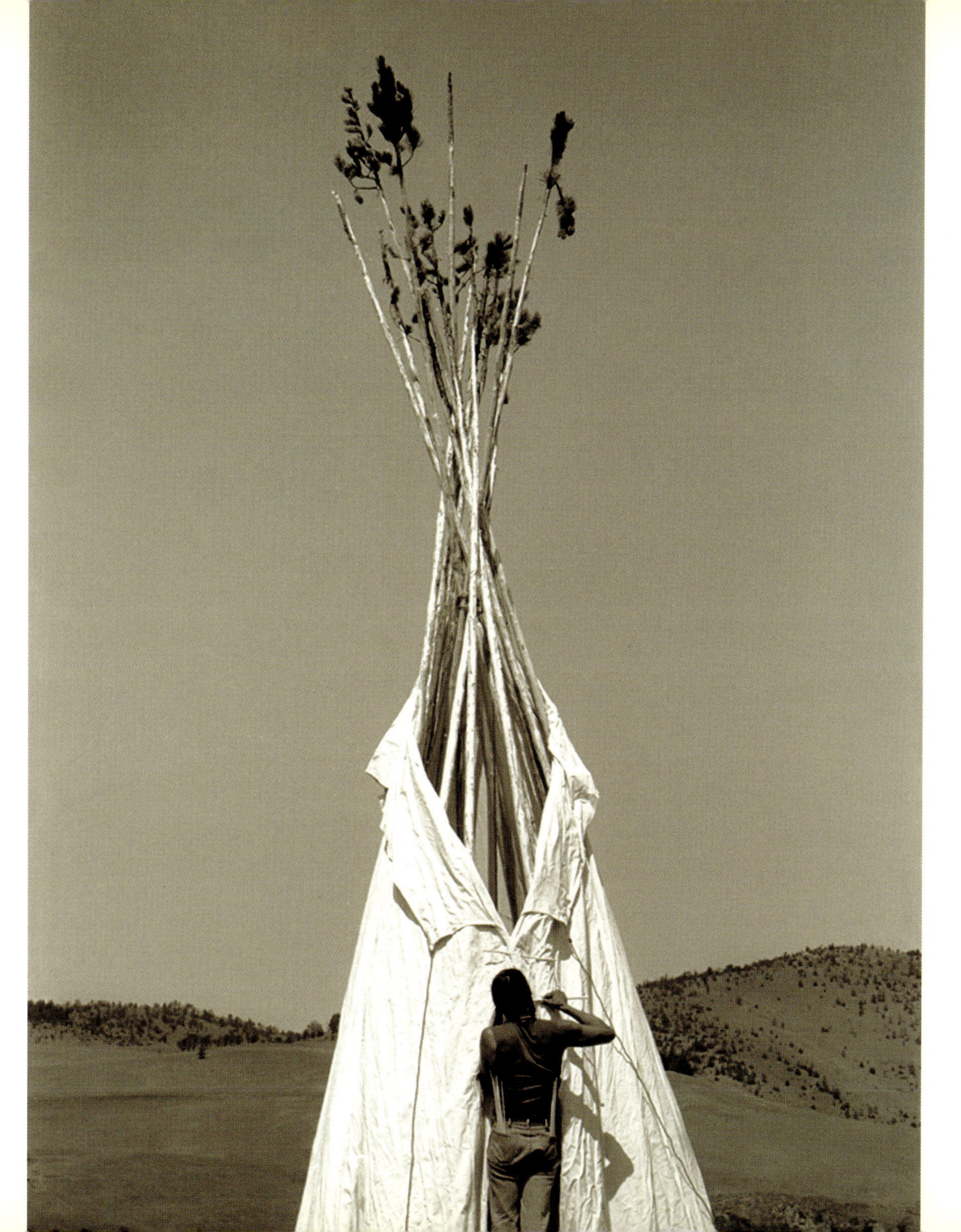

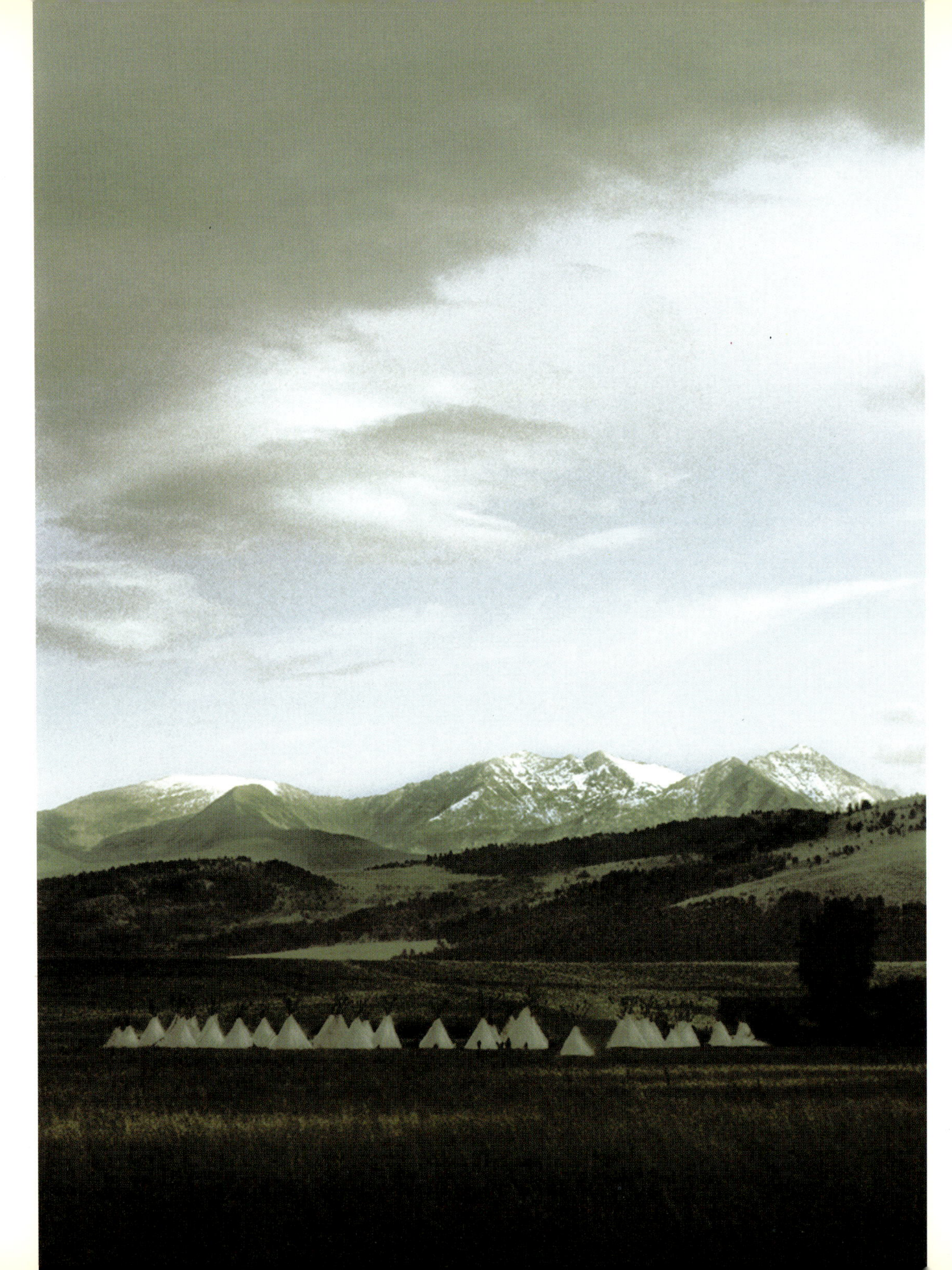

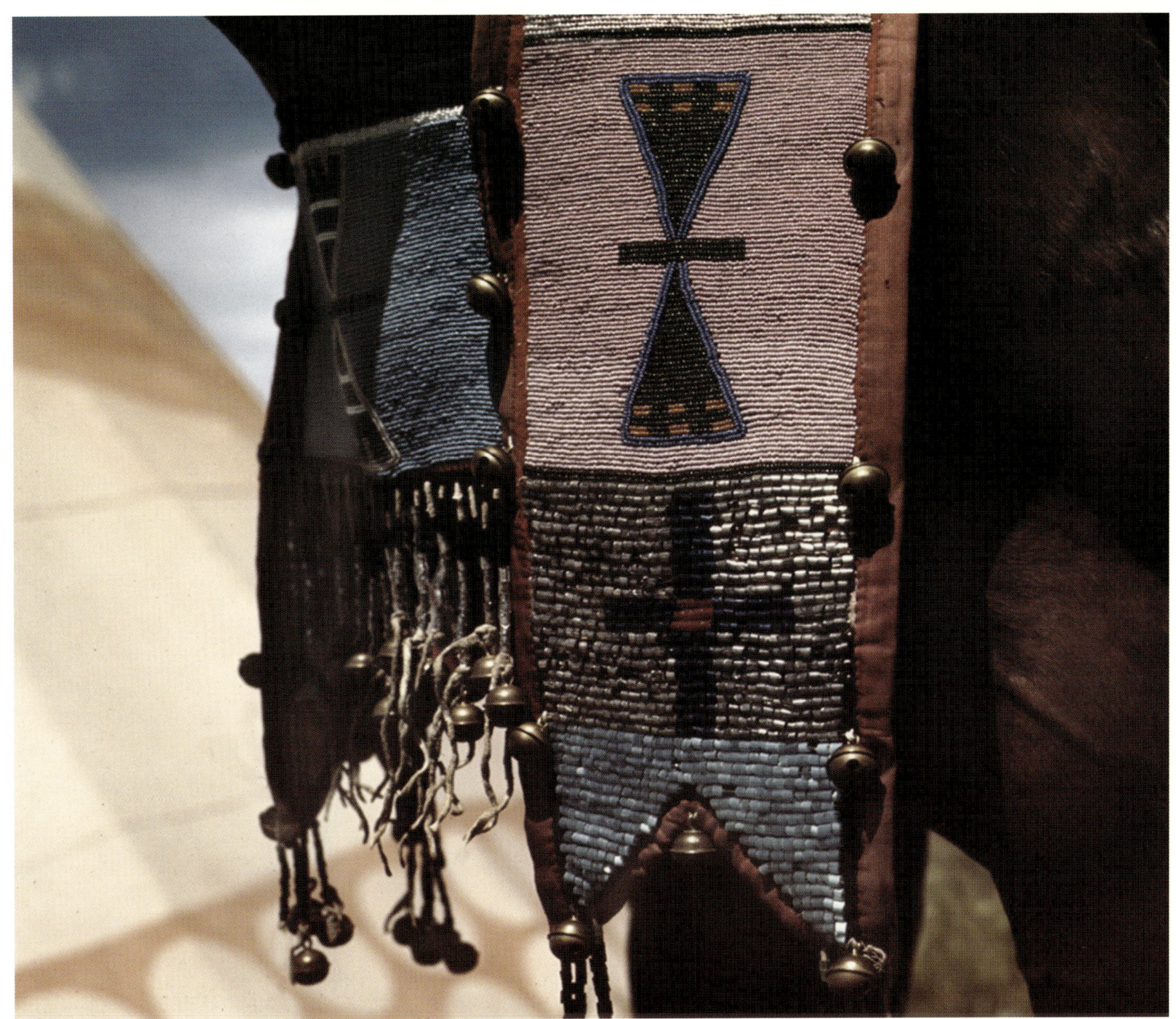

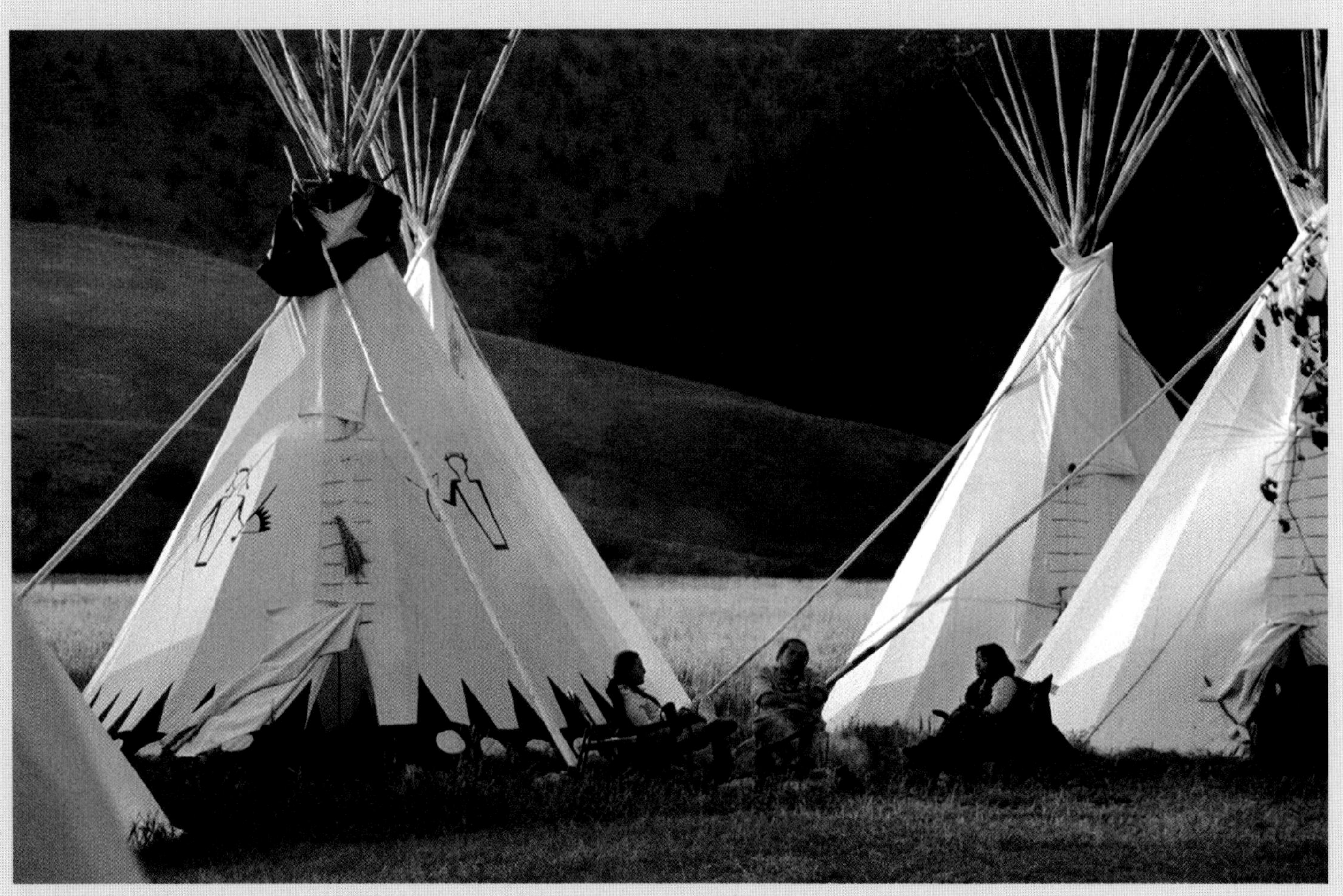

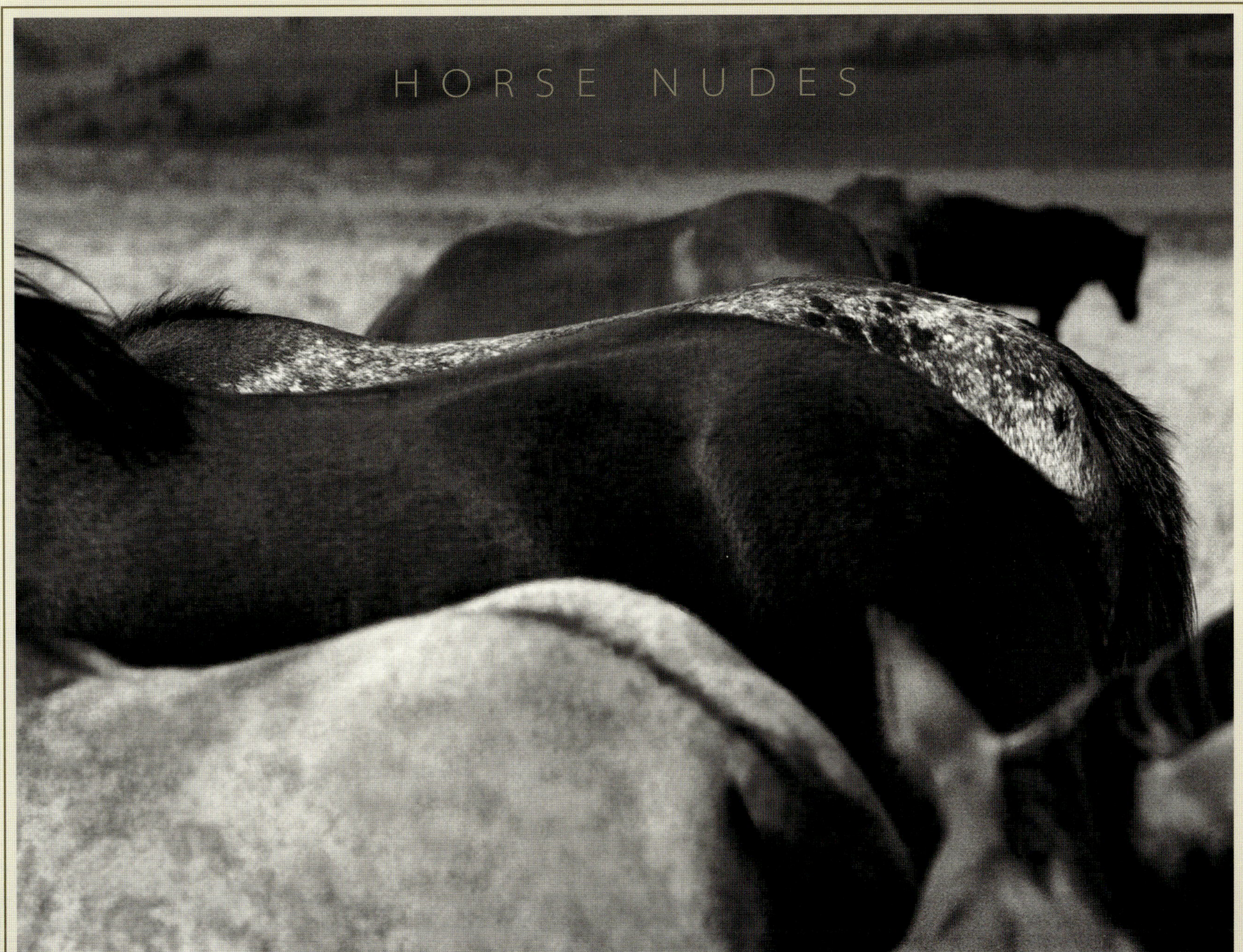
HORSE NUDES

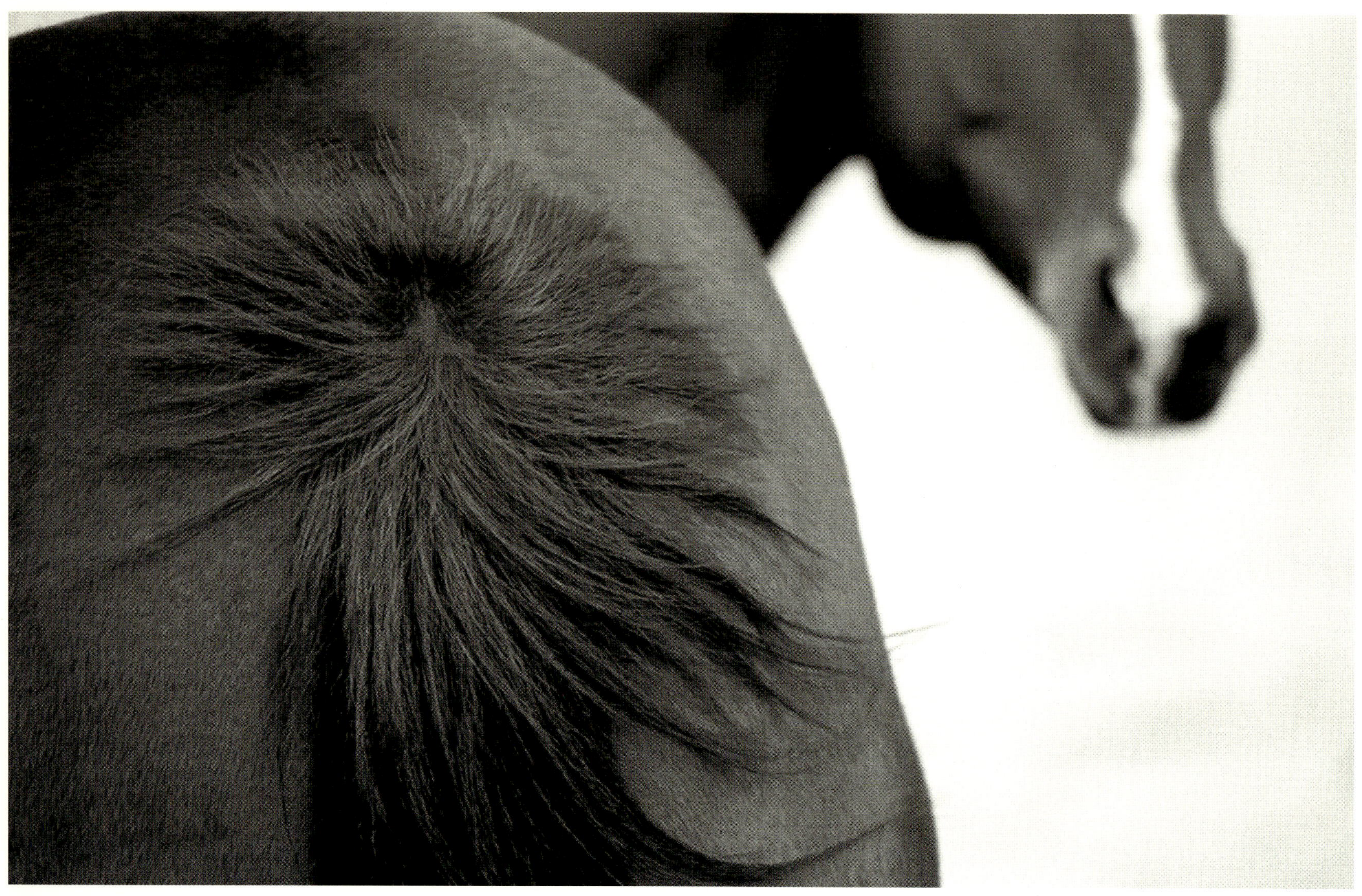

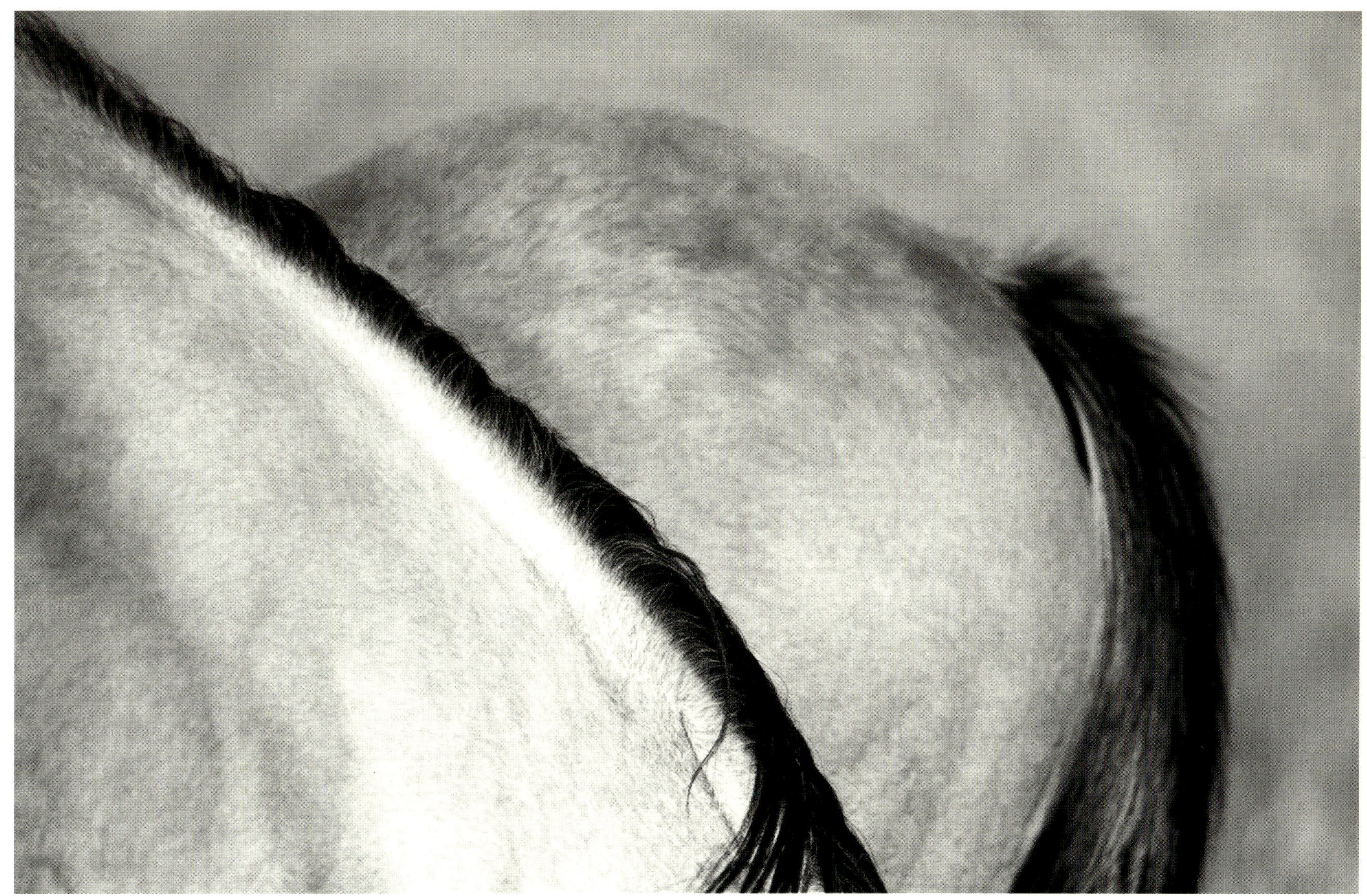

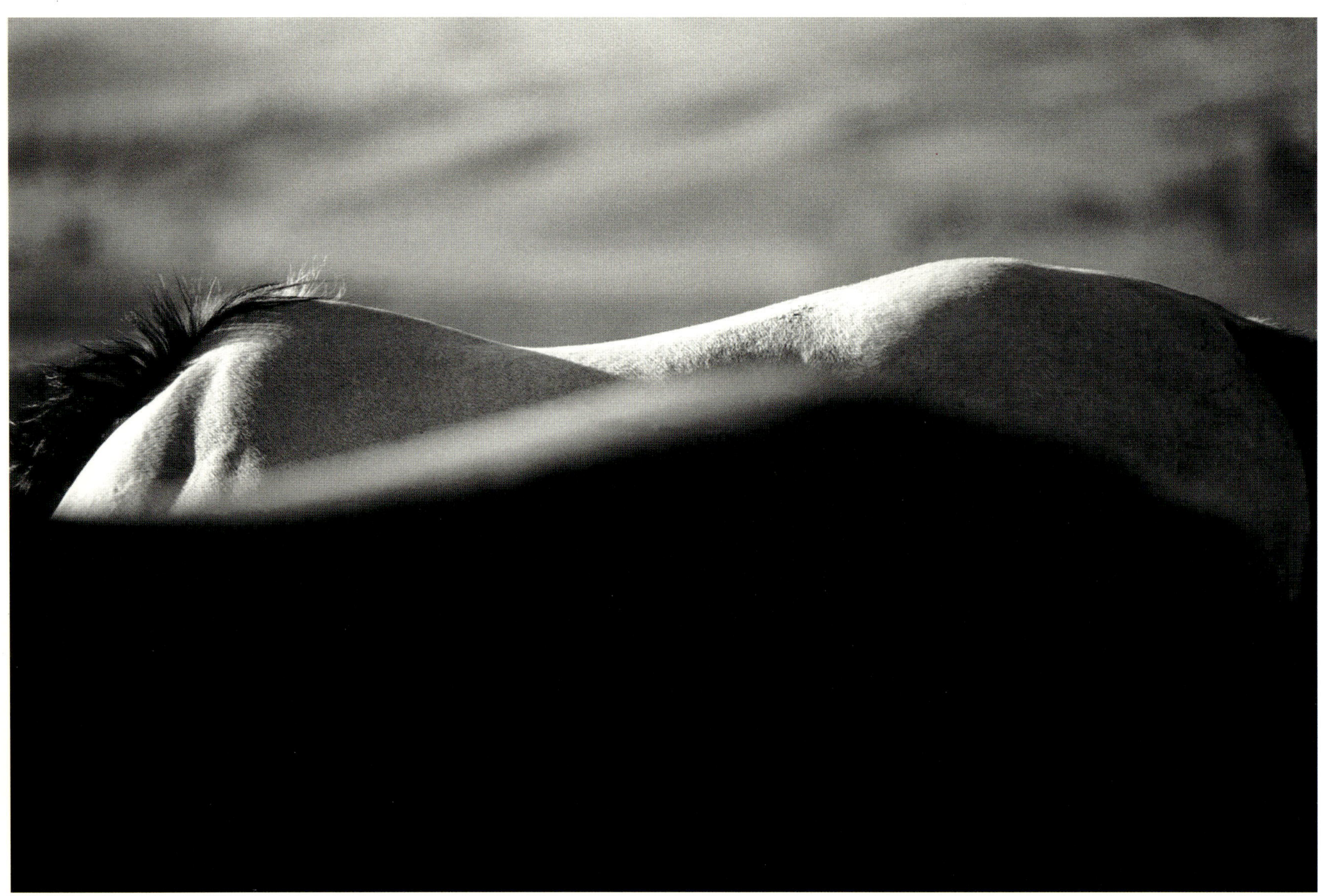

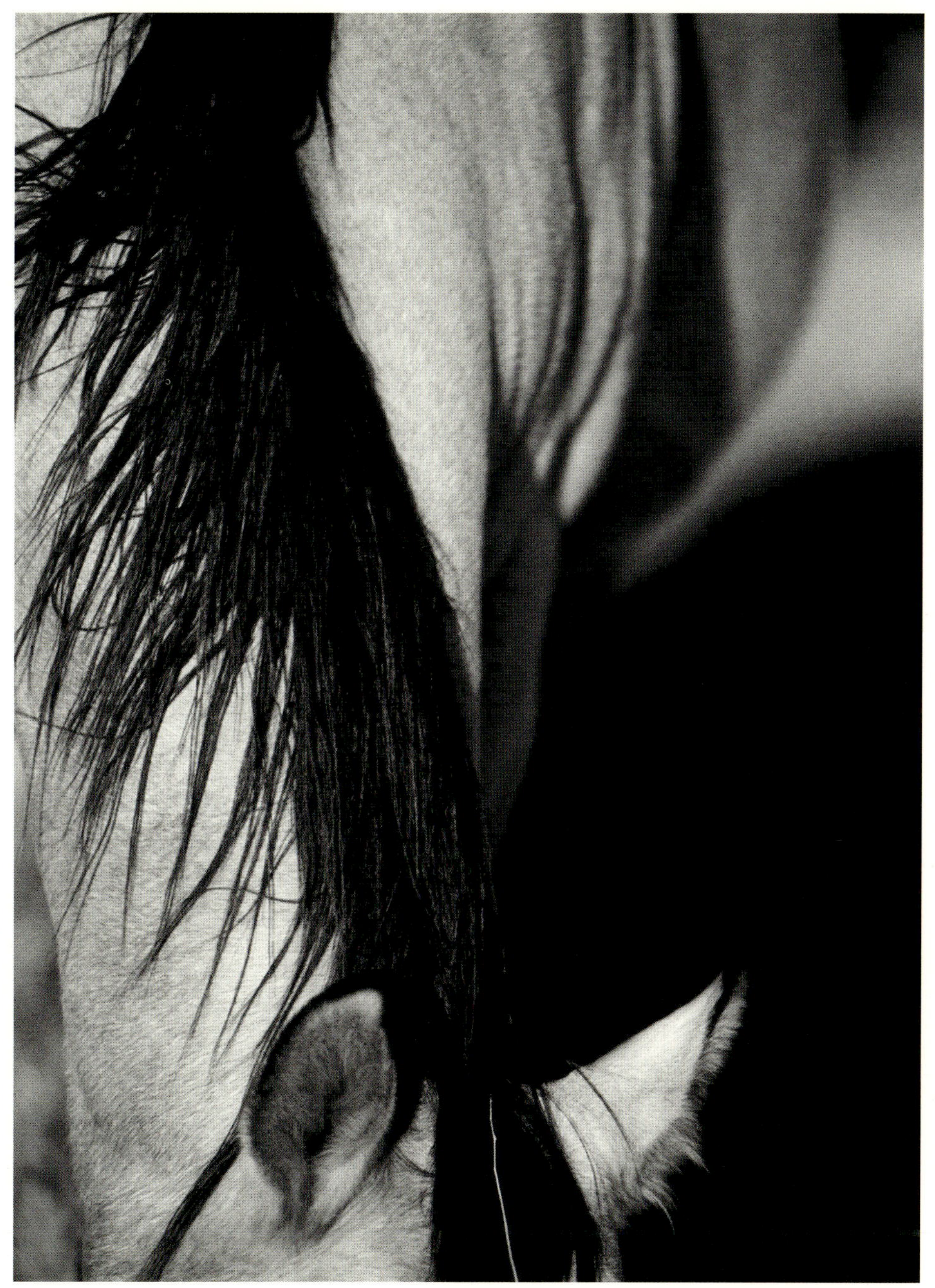

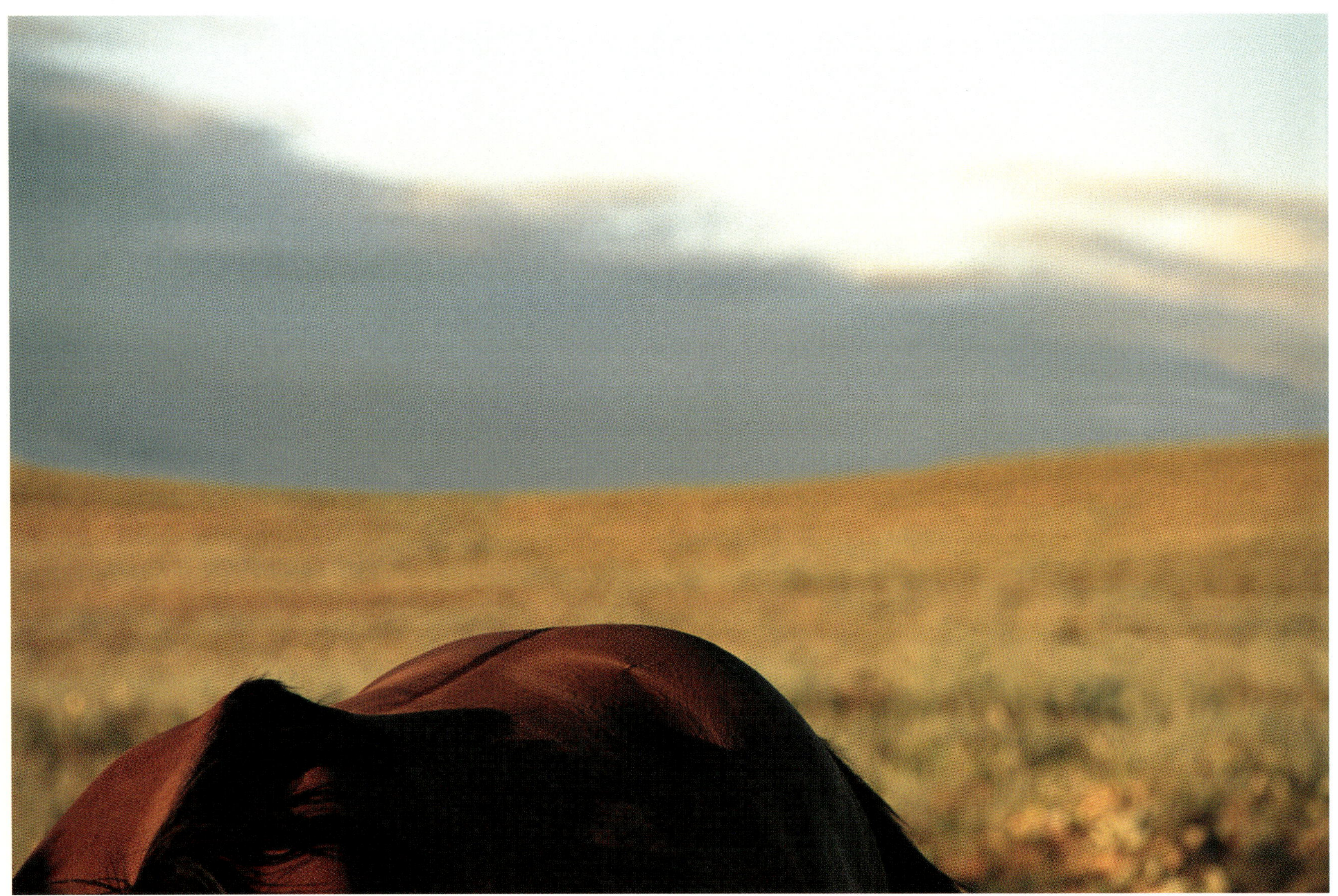

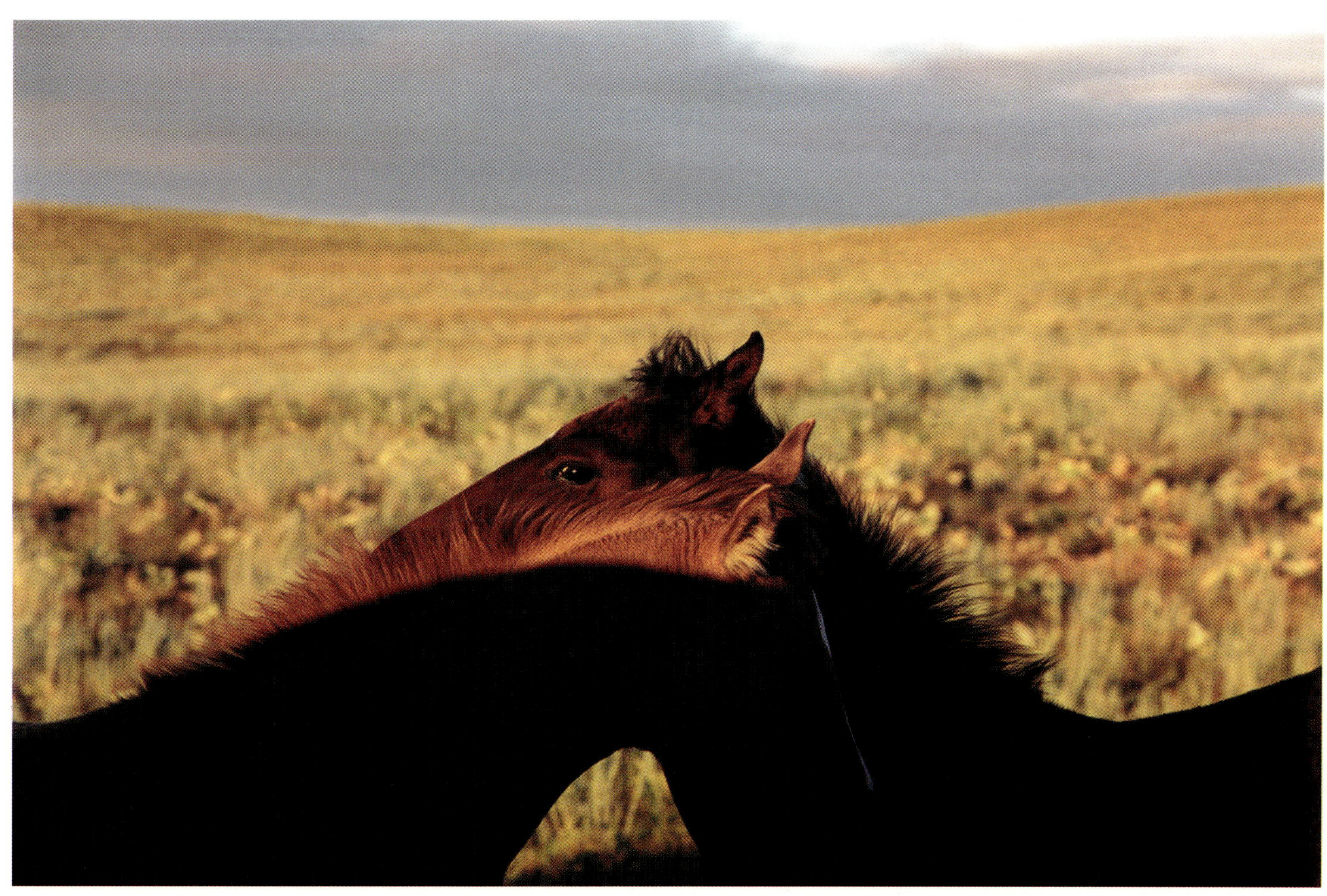

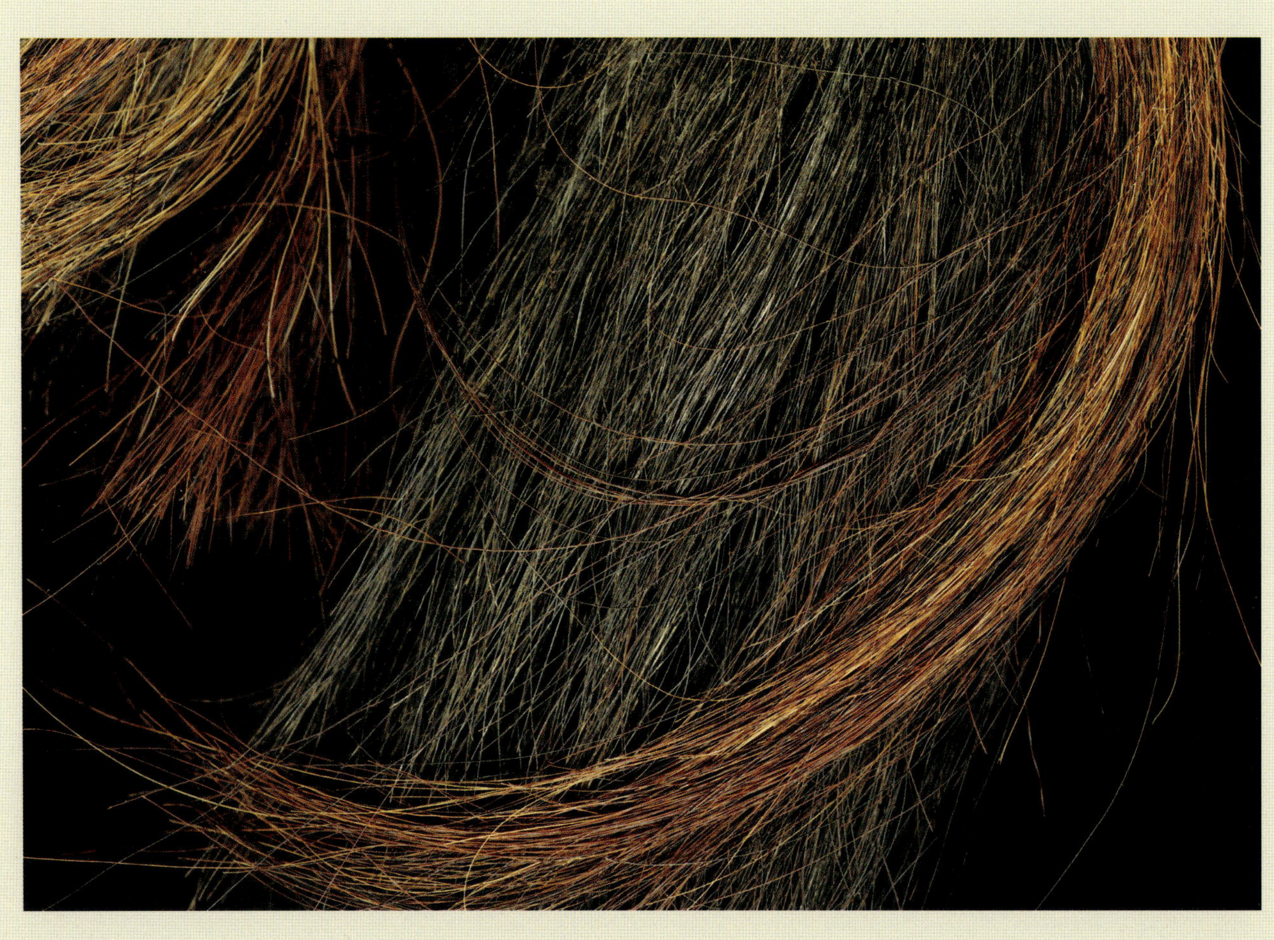

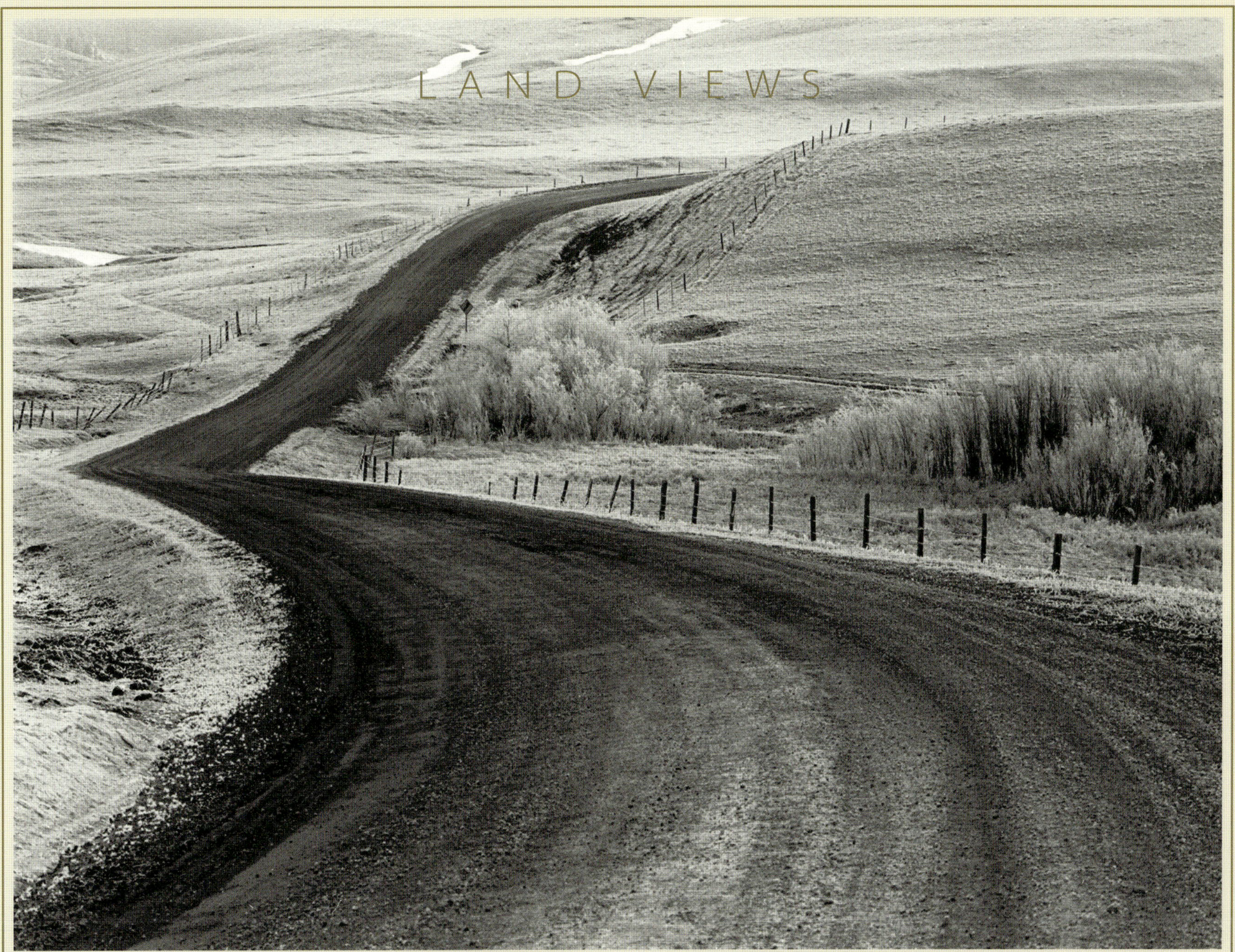
LAND VIEWS

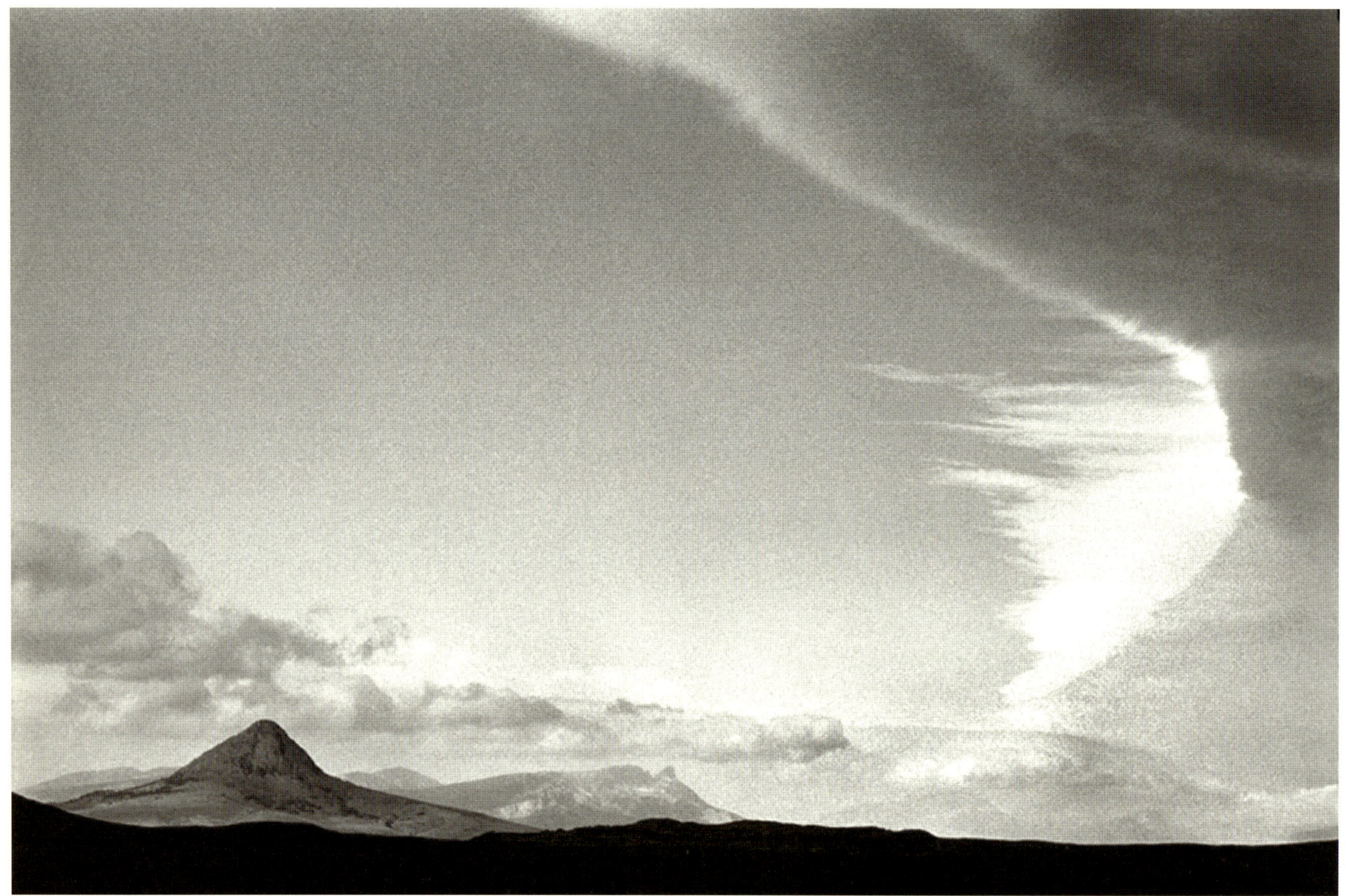

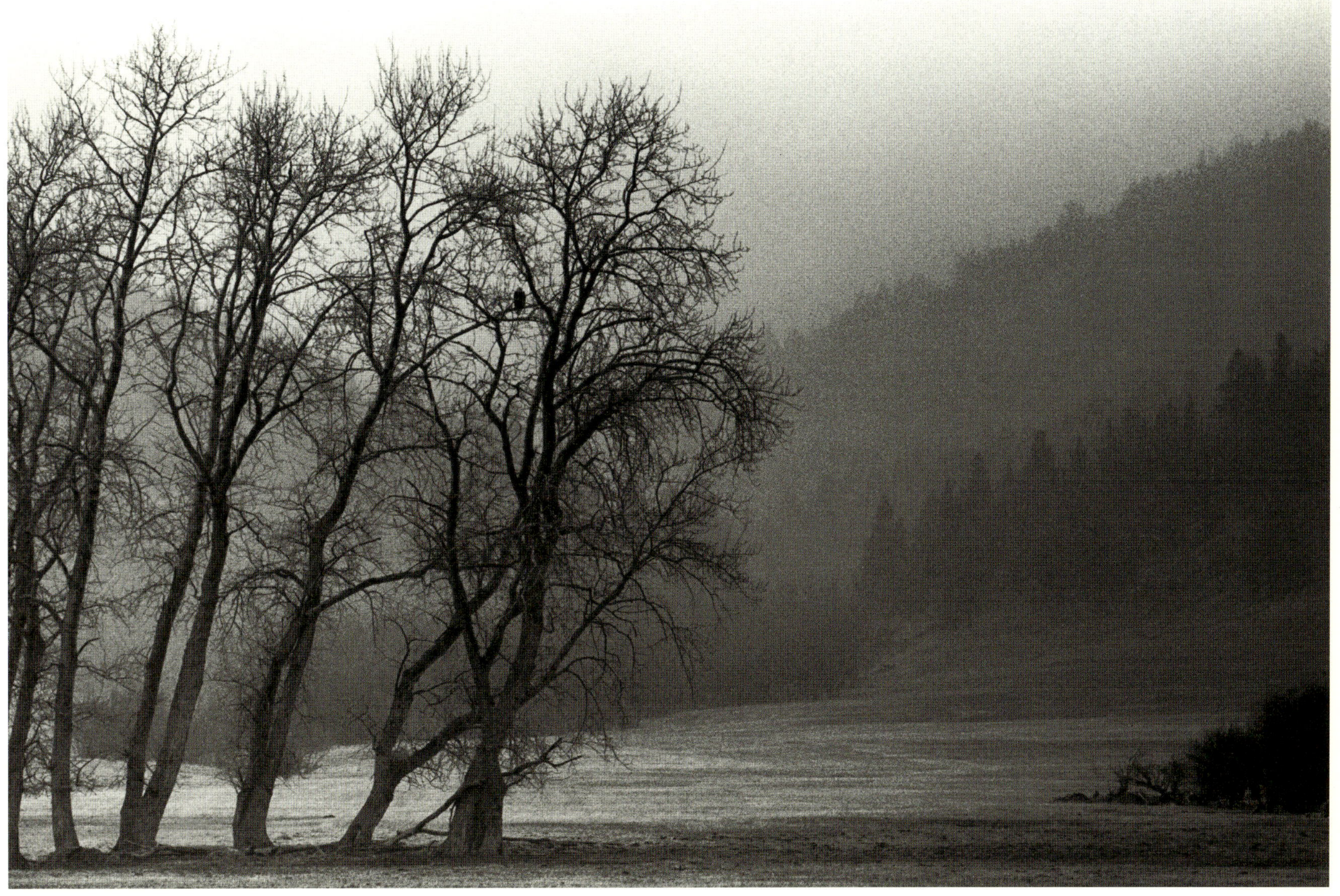

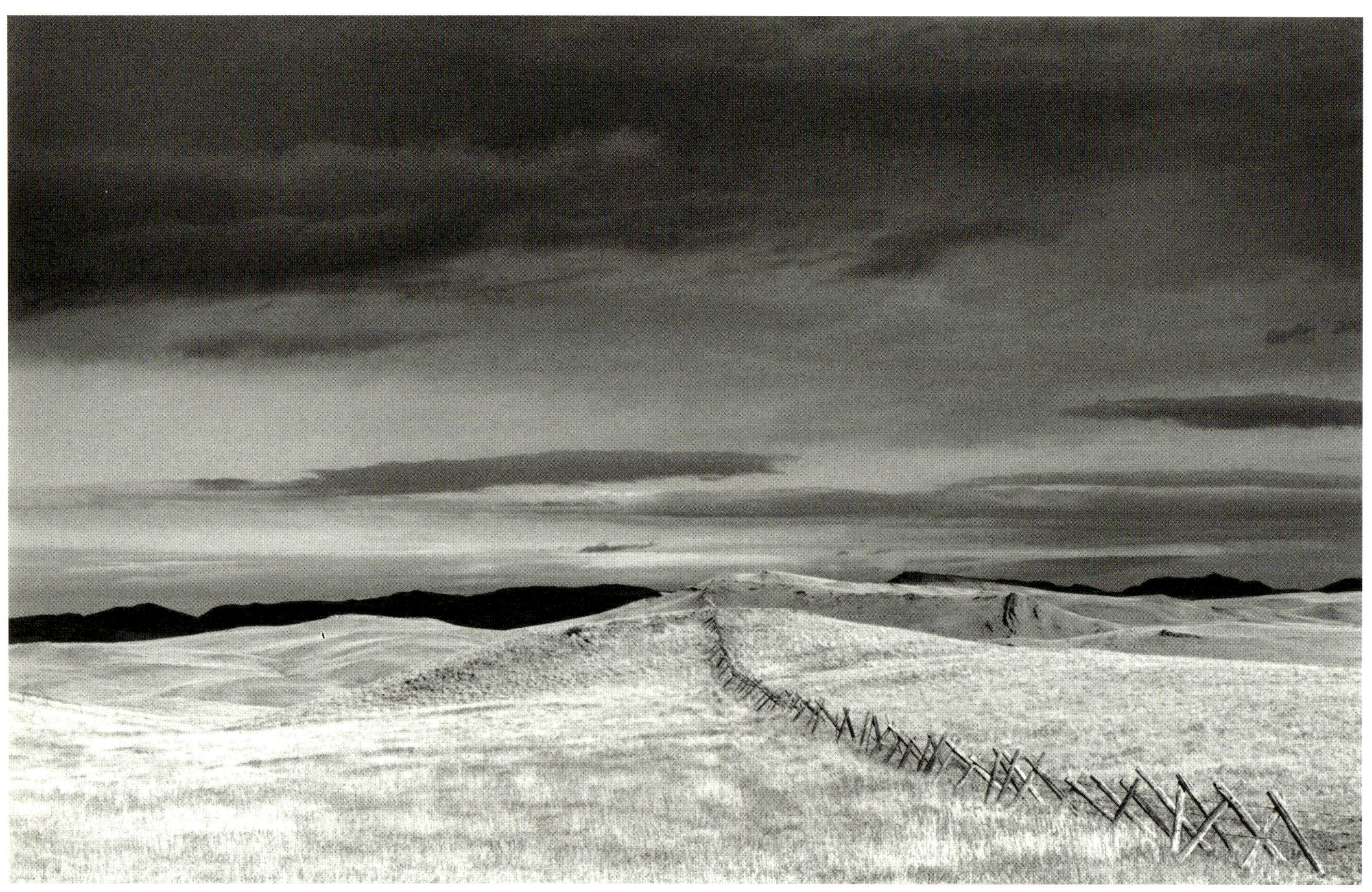

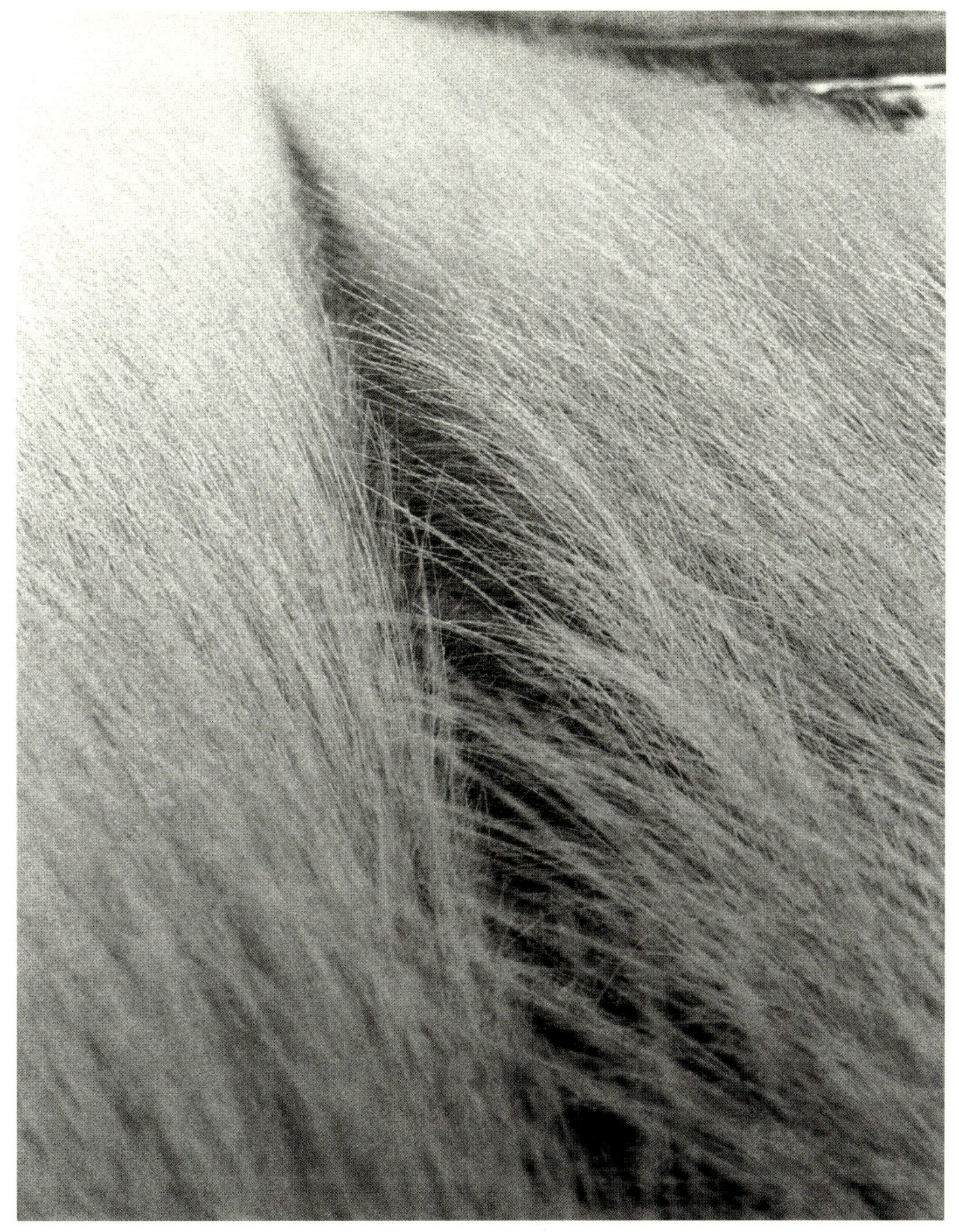

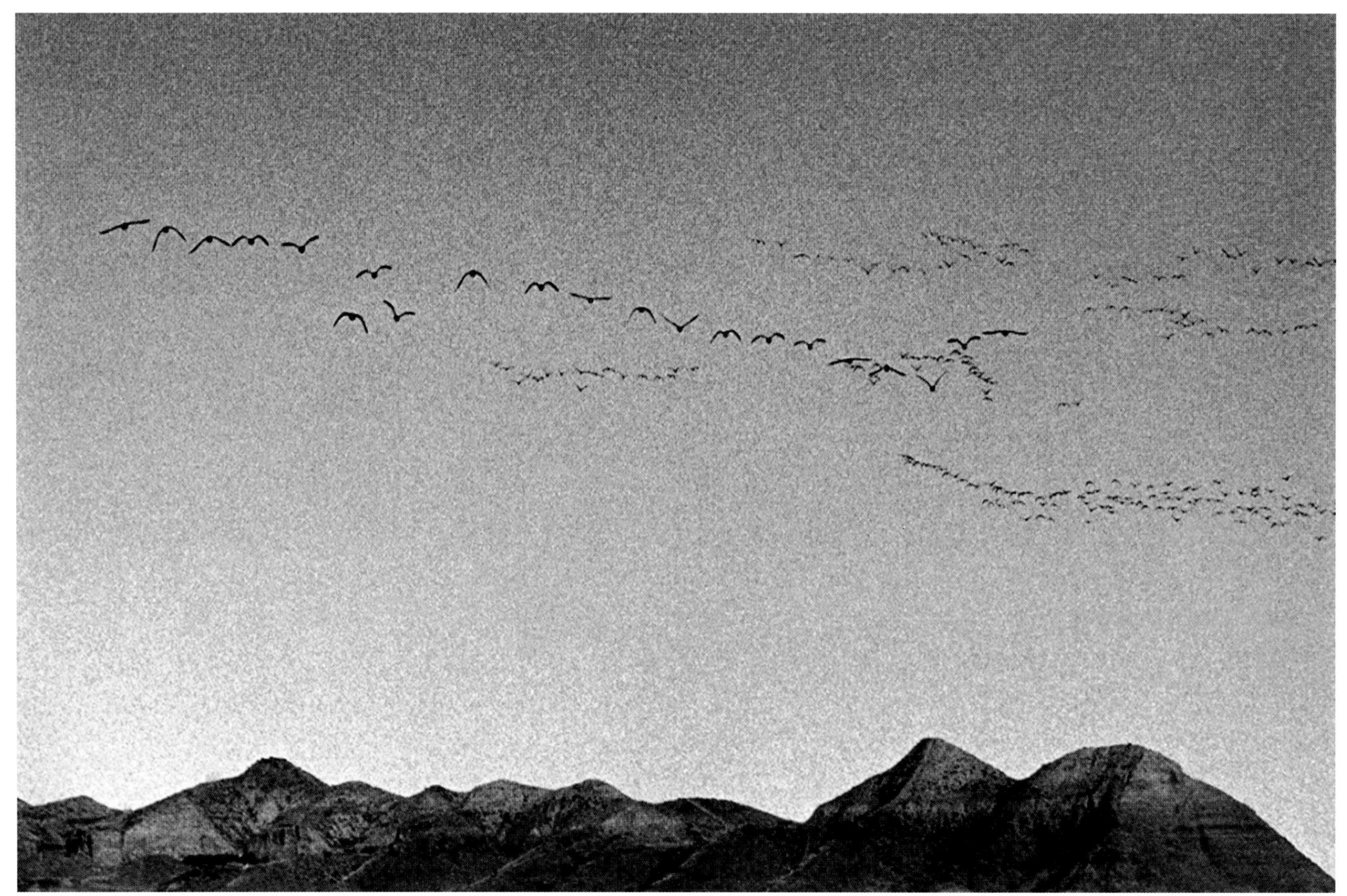

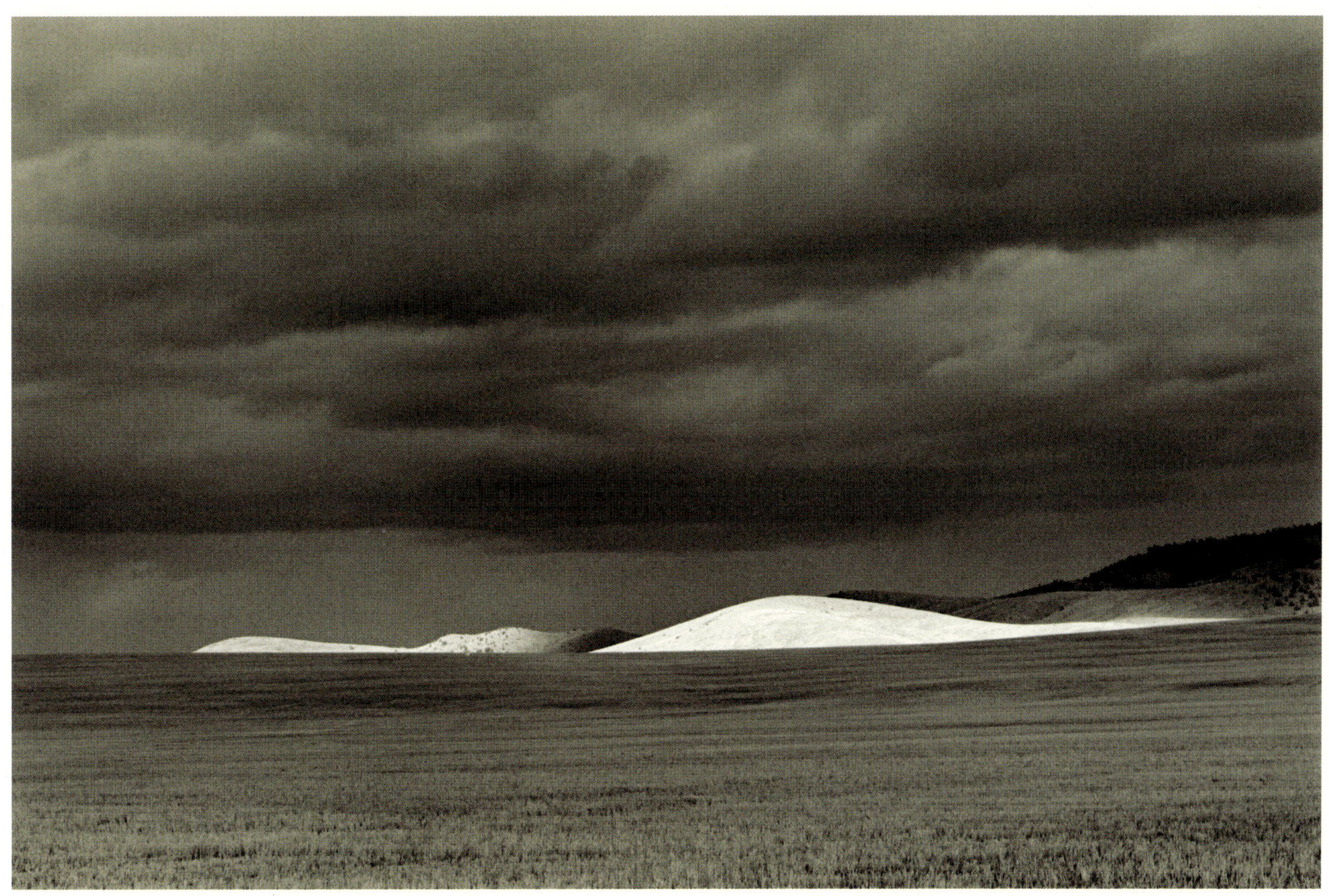

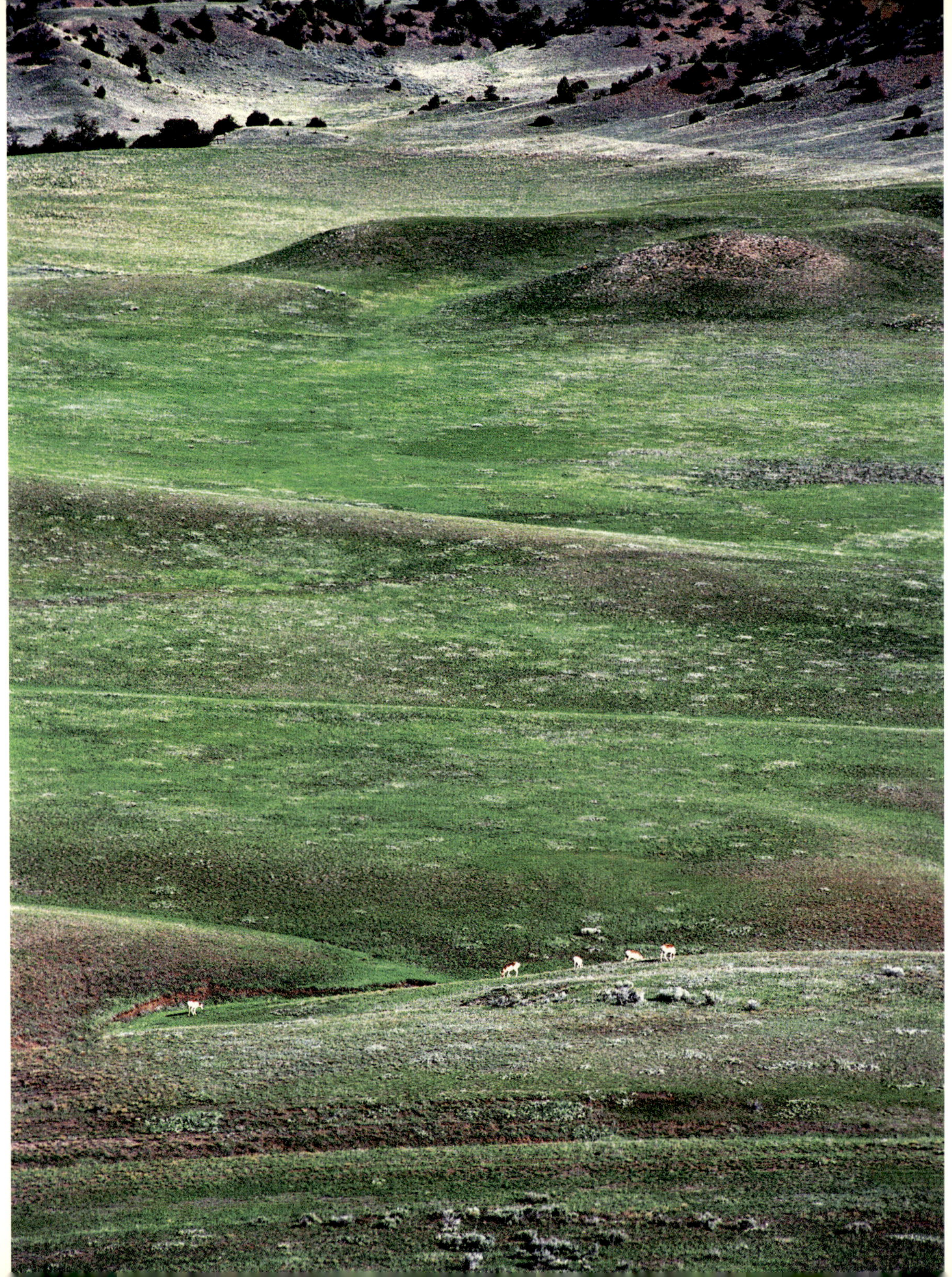

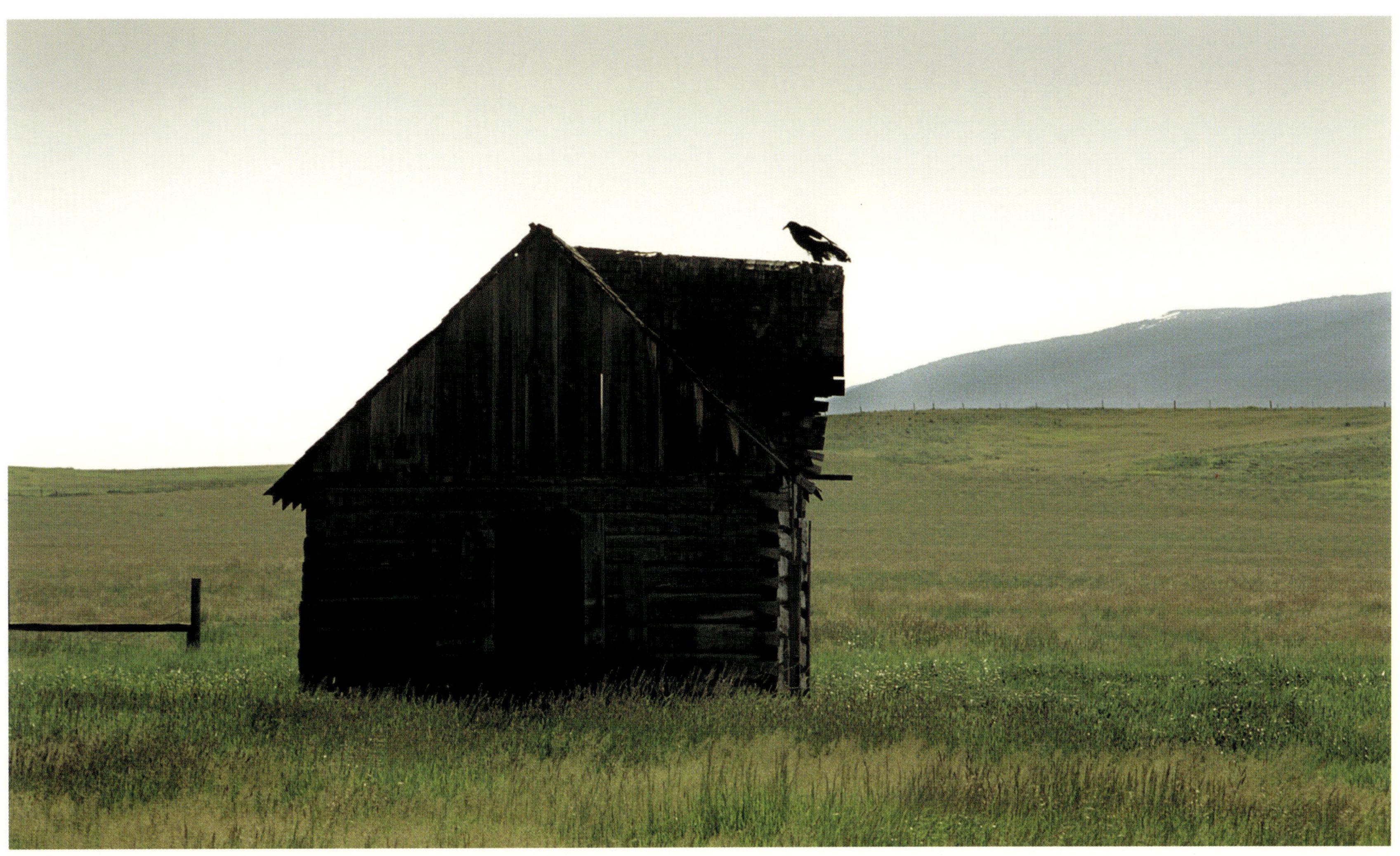

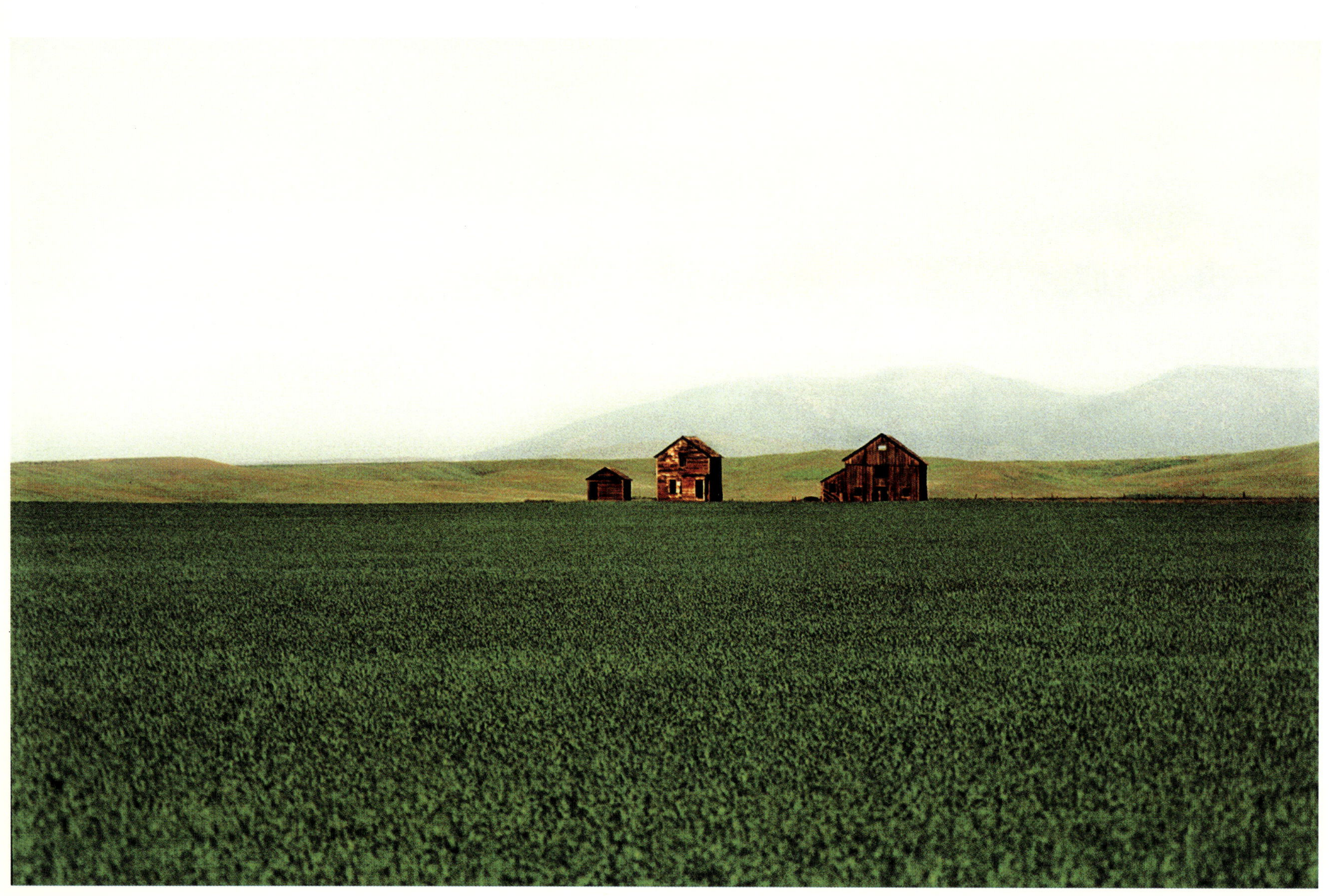

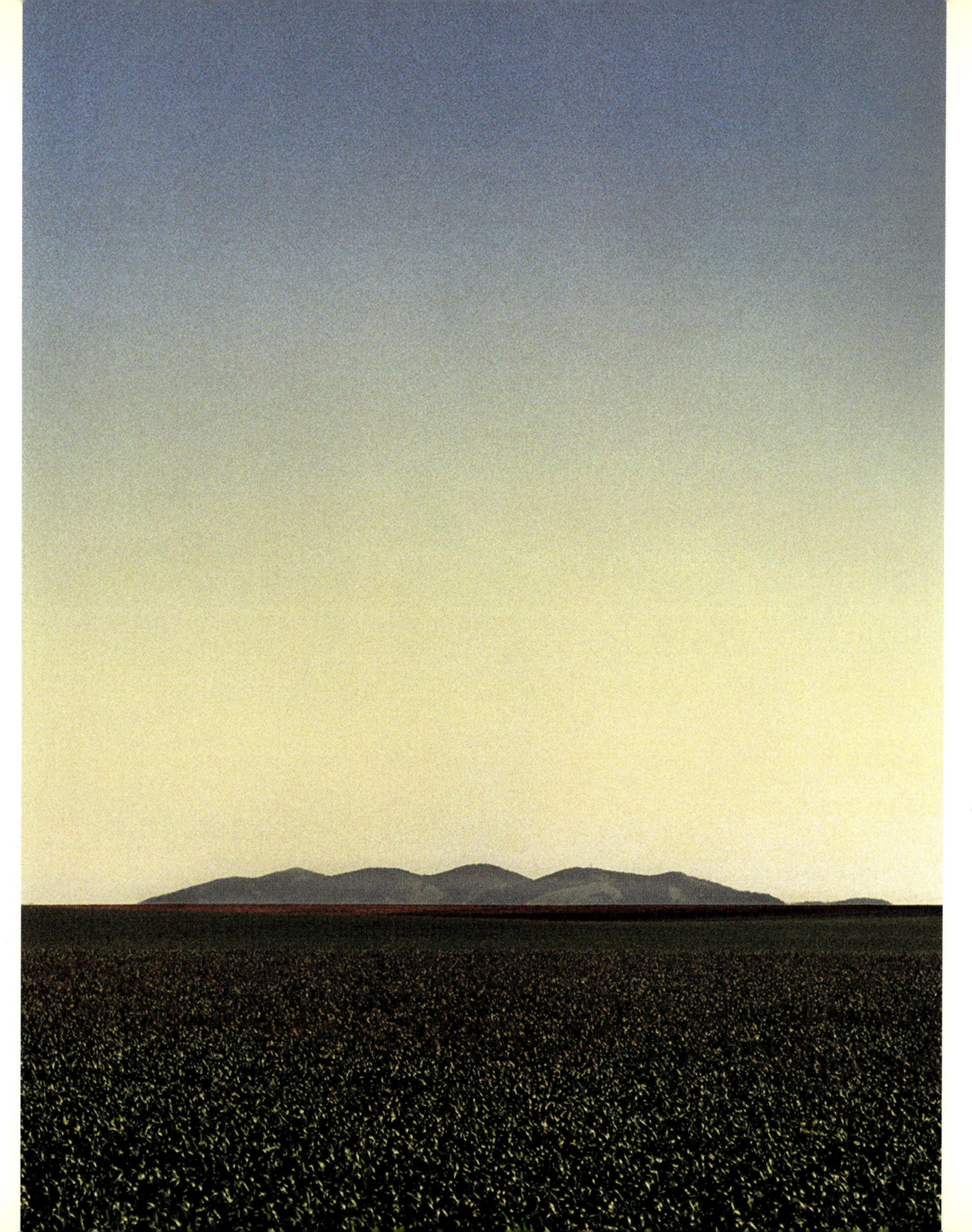

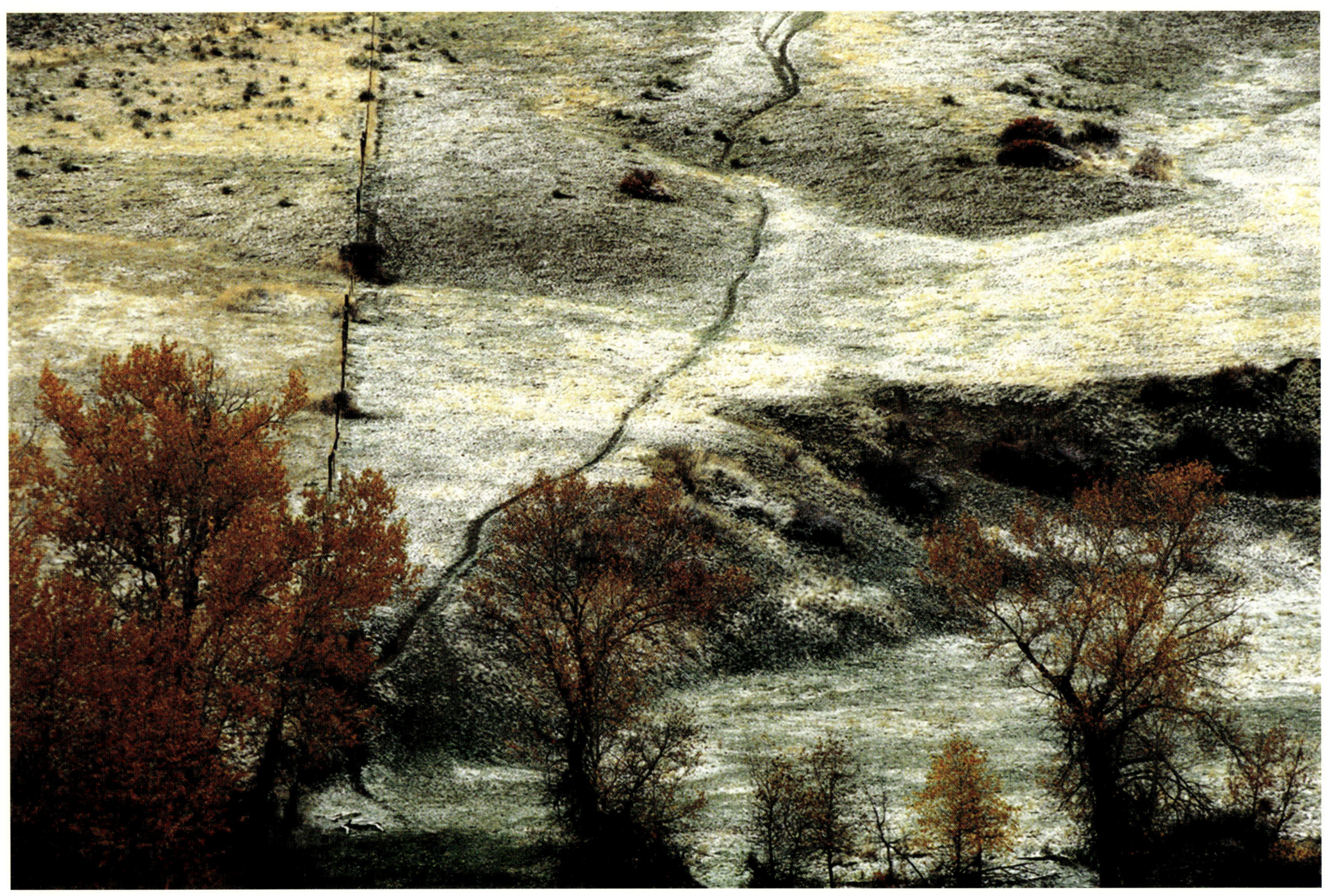

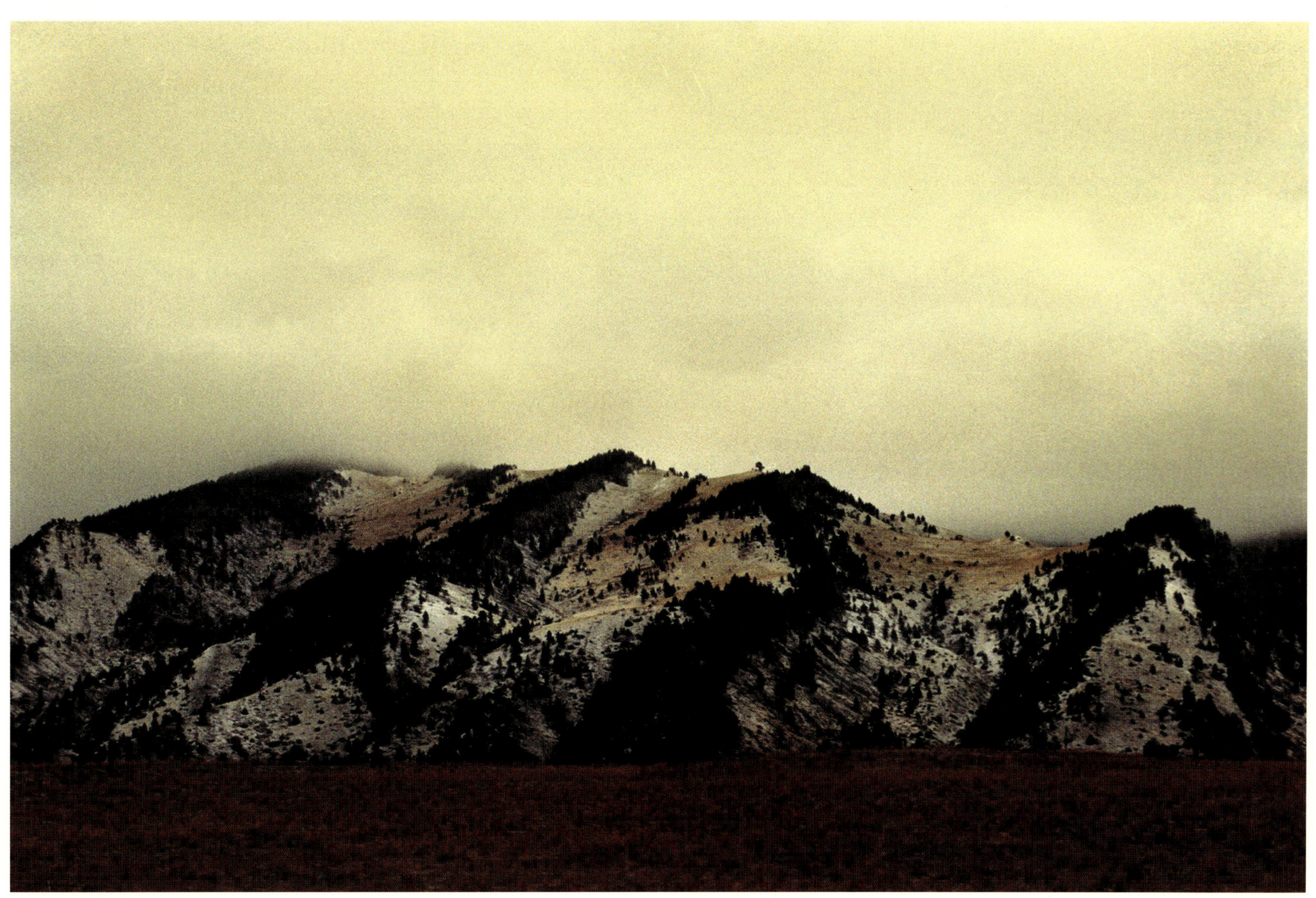

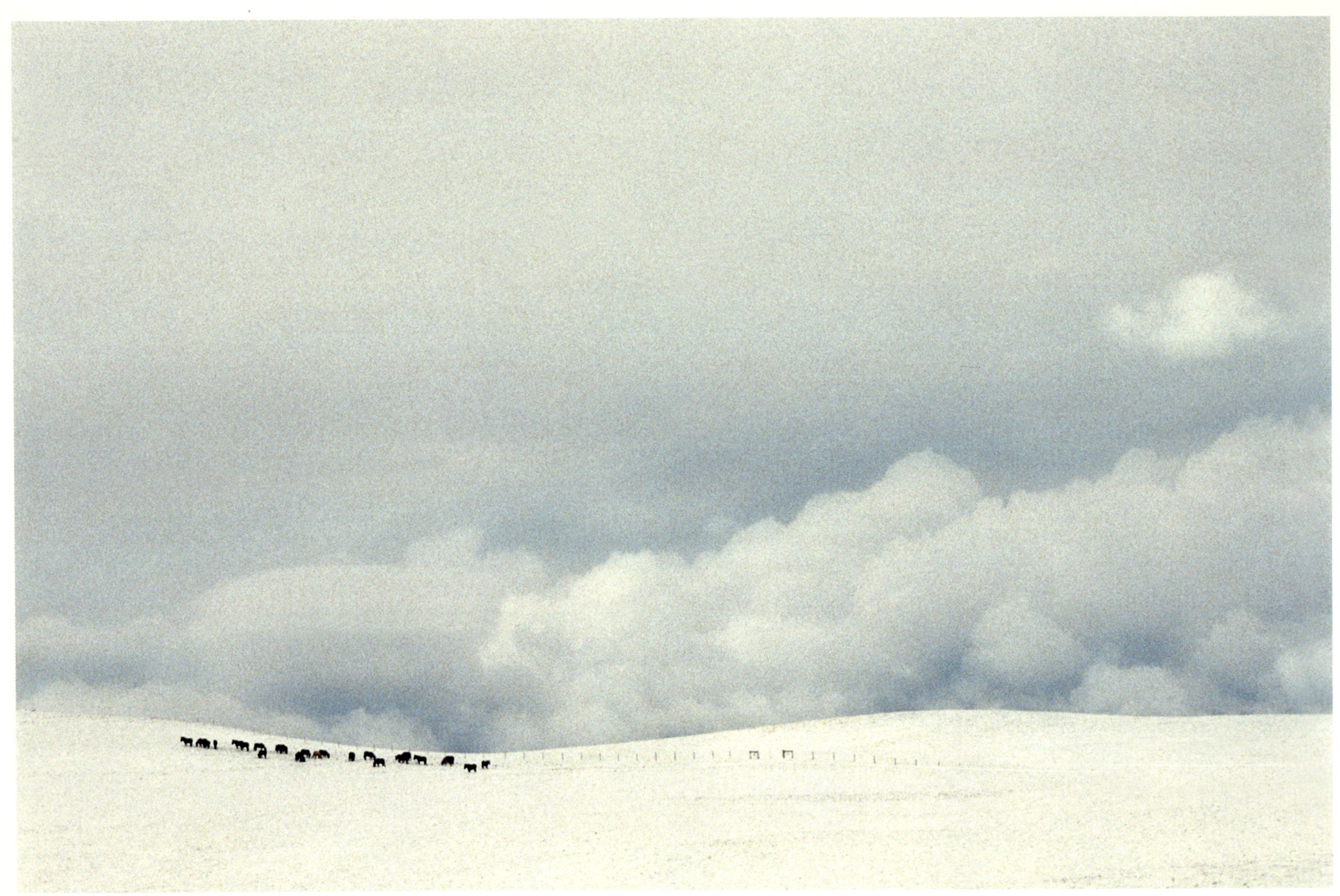

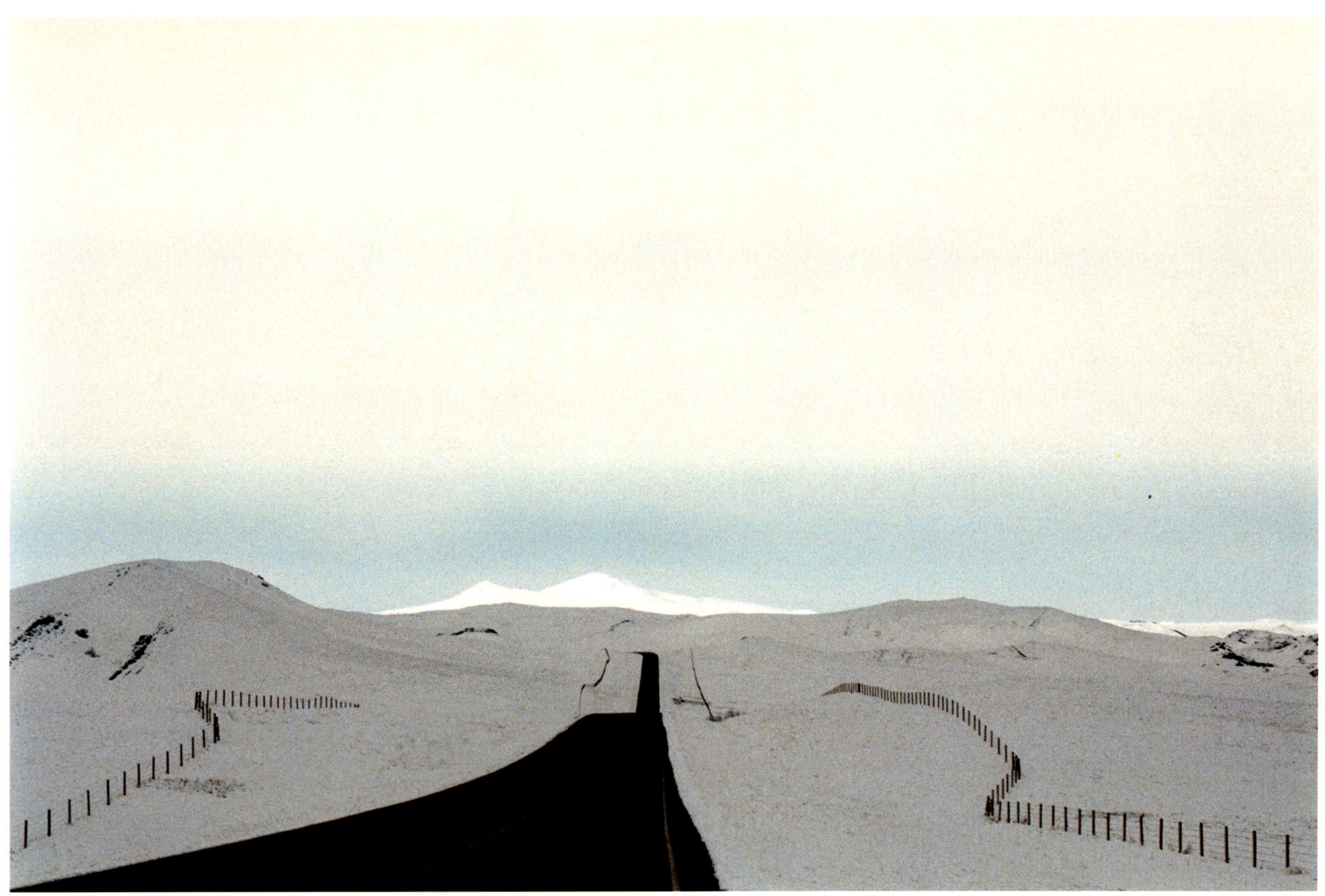

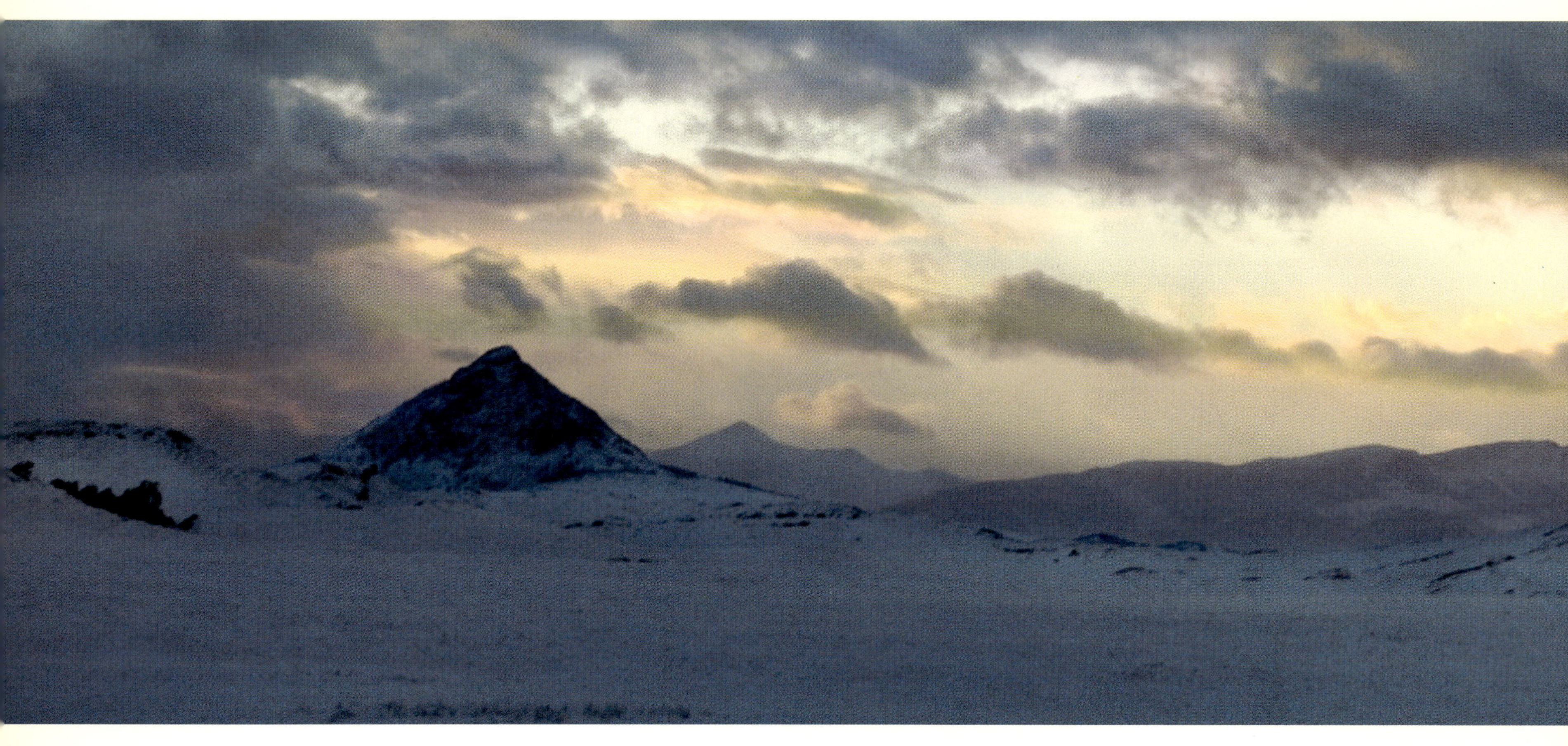

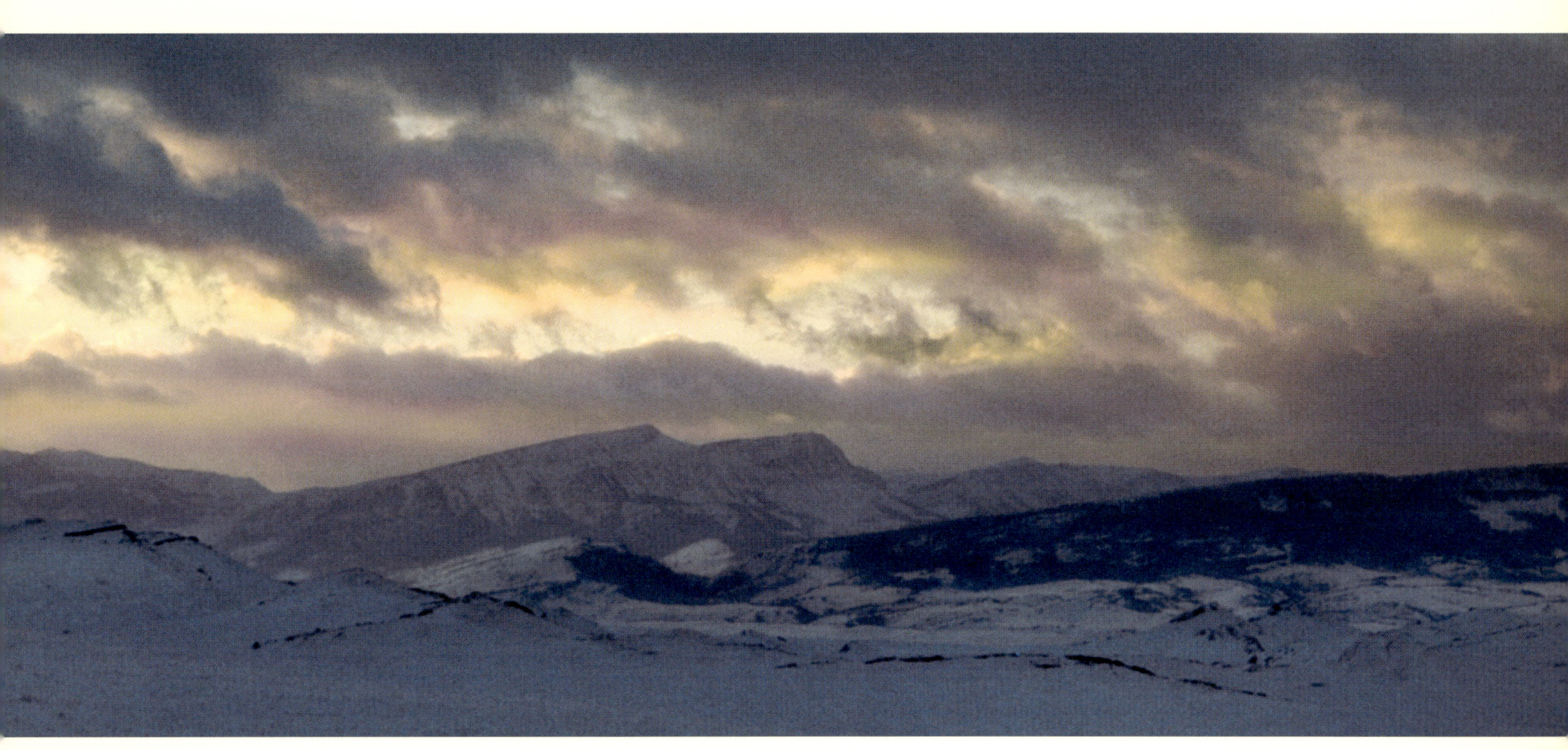

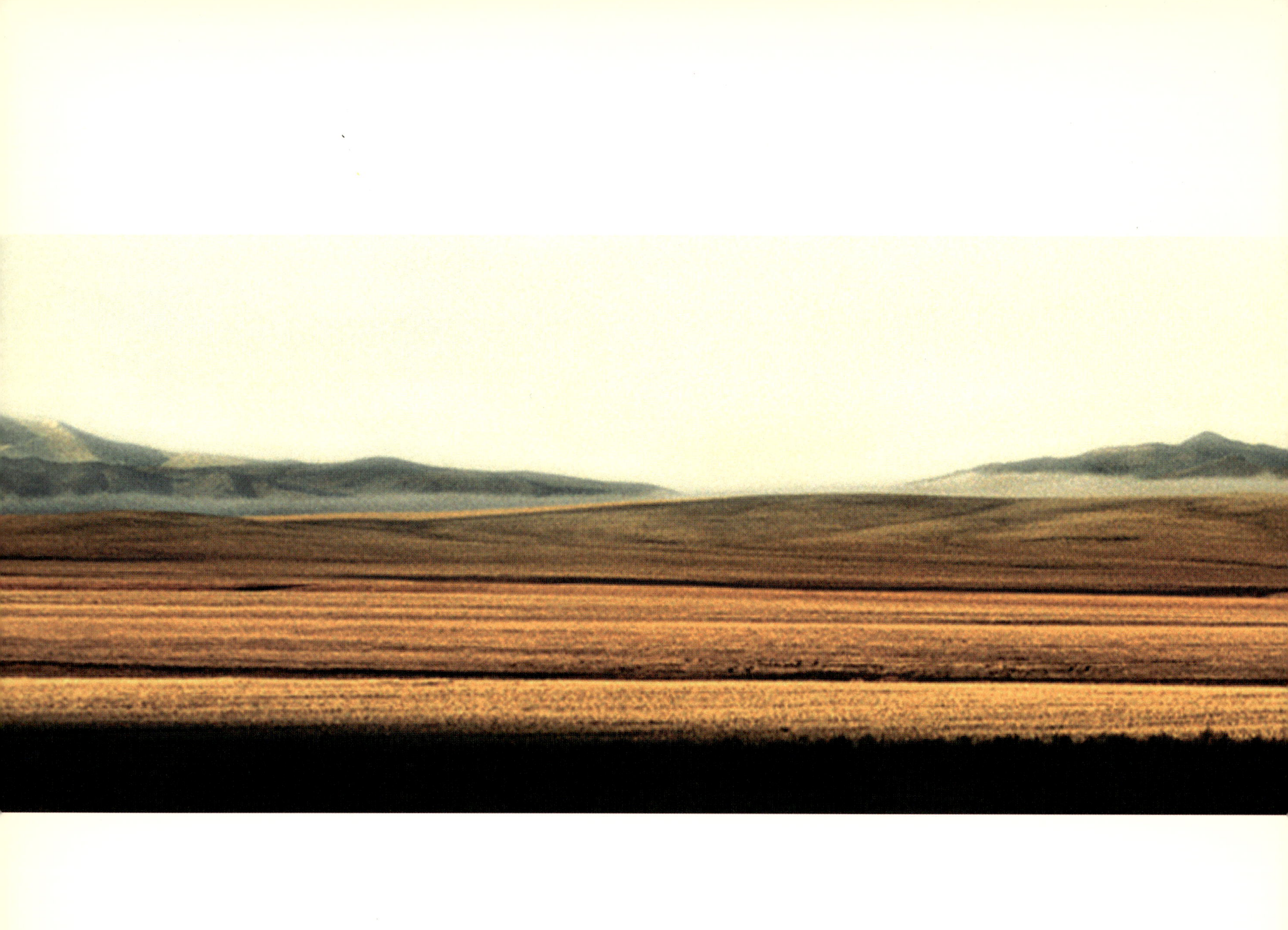

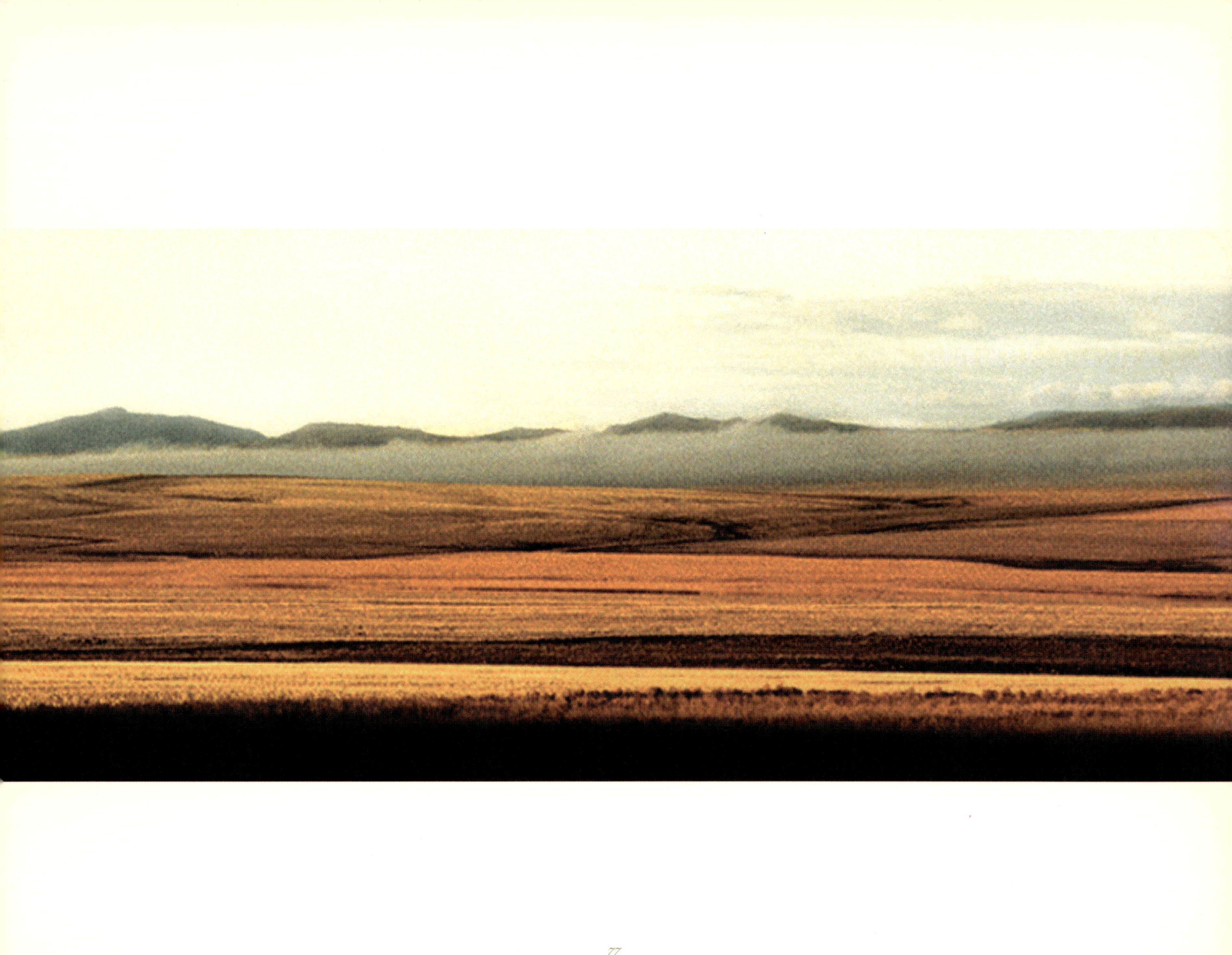

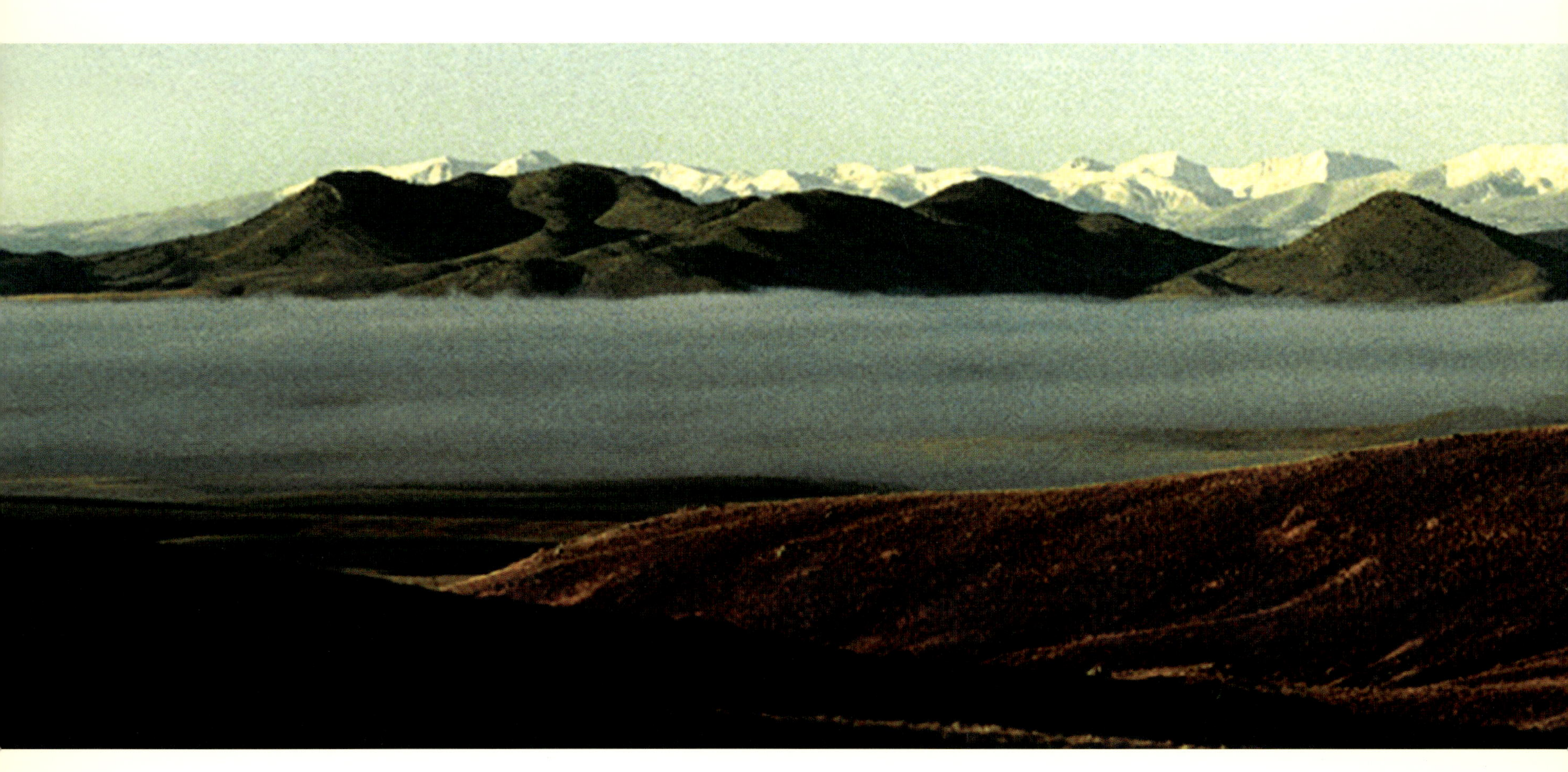

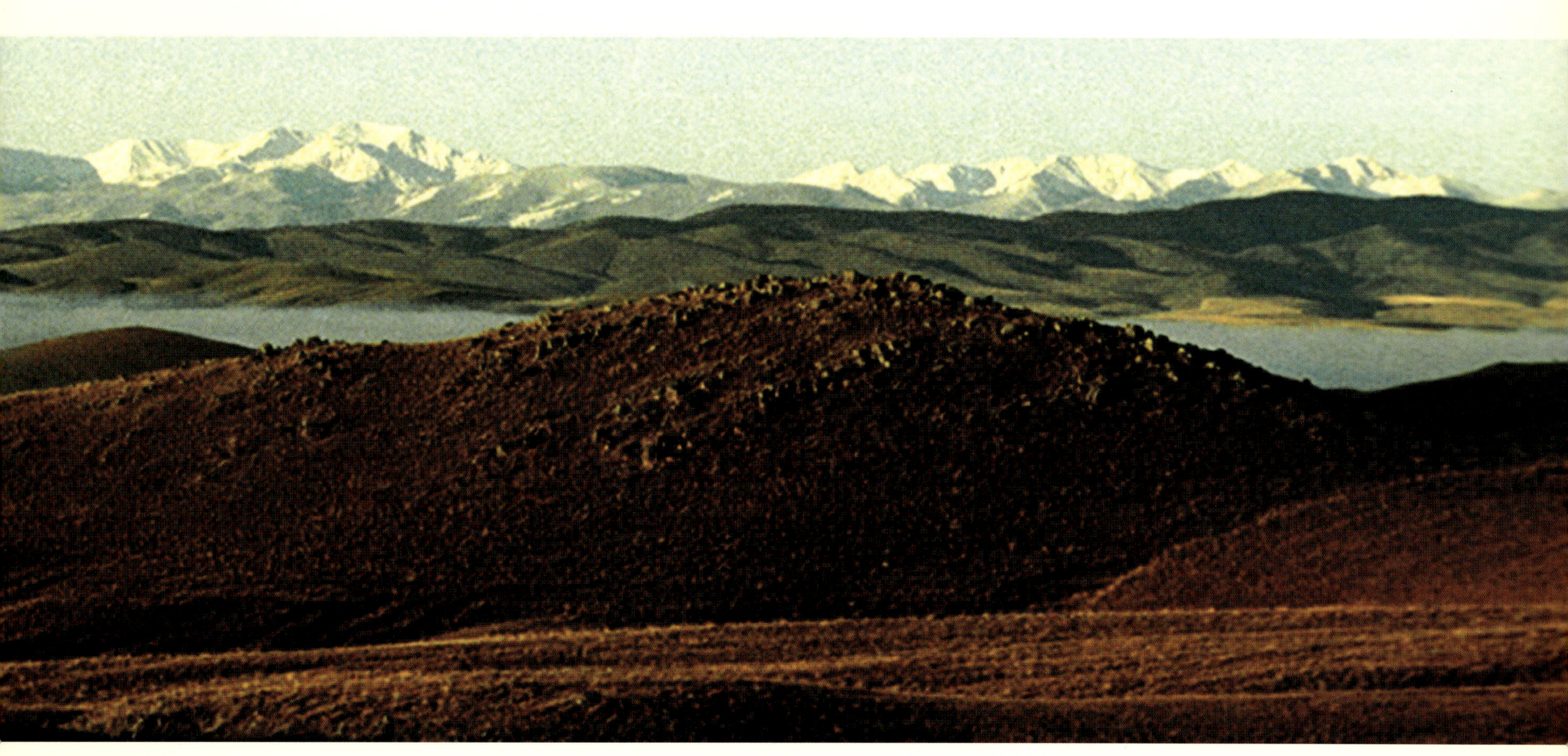

THE PLATES

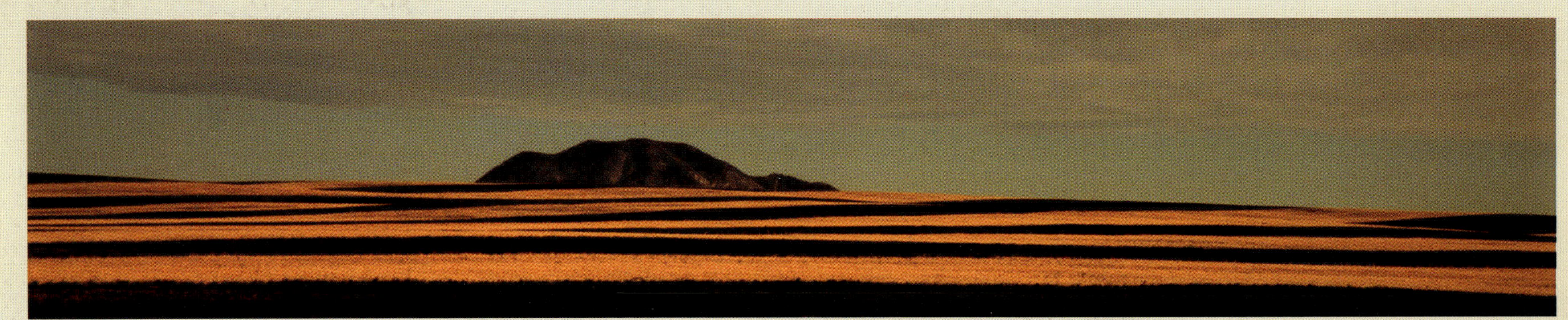